Romancing the Scone

Finding Our Way in a Land Full of Brits

By

Bill Leffler

D0067308

ISBN: 1-4033-9675-2 (e-book)
ISBN: 1-4033-9676-0 (Paperback)

Library of Congress Control Number: 2002095994

This book is printed on acid free paper.

Printed in the United States of America
Bloomington, IN

1stBooks - rev. 01/03/03

Prologue

In a surge of elemental gusto, Tawny raced toward the sound of the huntsman's horn, directly at a menacingly tall stone barricade. I watched a dozen other hunters ahead of us clear it. With not one clue about my role in this impending act of lunacy, I leaned forward, grabbed the saddle front, and let Tawny have her head. Five meters in front of the wall we went airborne, cutting off a redcoated rider who reined his horse to the right, passionately venting a barrage of verbal abuse at us.

Chasing a fox, I found out, has varying degrees of risk, especially if a tall leap in a single bound presents an impossible challenge. A wooden fence, in that case, will probably give way, unable to withstand the momentum of a ton of horse and human flesh. Hedgerows will give way too, though a certain amount of contusion and abrasion ensues. But to the mounted horseman who would otherwise be an irresistible force, a dry-stone wall can present an immovable object.

Despite the wisdom that allegedly accrues to a geriatric, Tawny understood none of this. For an indefinite period Tawny and I glided, first in suspended animation, then in free fall At that point I also found out that the leap is only half the hazard – landing is the remainder. Tawny's abrupt contact with the ground occurred at the moment that I hovered about six inches above the saddle. Over her head I vaulted. My only recollection for the next few moments was the redcoat whose jump we had interrupted, smirking as he bounded by.

After a quick inventory of my extremities, I realized that lush grass and mud had cushioned my ignoble landing. I rolled over to one side to let twenty or thirty more riders carry on, following Tawny, who had not paused a moment.

Within a few moments, a horse and rider that seemed to have been launched sideways appeared over the wall. The rider flailed at the air in a vain attempt to right the two of them. Horse and rider crashed to the ground, with the latter skidding the ten meters to me, stopping face down, still. The horse scrambled to its feet and with an embarrassed glance trotted off in the direction of the others.

"Are you okay?" I tried.

"Bugger-all if I know," came the answer from the motionless form. "But we'll survive, what?"

He rolled over carefully. "No sense whinging over spilt milk. Or should I say a spilt rider? Ha. Des Manning," he said, holding out his right hand while producing a silver flask with his left from his tunic. "Would you care for a dram of gin?"

Bugger-all is right, I thought between sips. Yet another quintessentially unflappable Brit.

1

In the Land of Gazumping

"Brilliant choice of yours, renting this house. You know why they called it Michael Court?"

Our effervescent landlord, Stephanie, waited for our response like a panting collie ready to chase a thrown ball. We had just now met her for the first time at the front door to our home in Surrey, England, amidst boxes, crates, and the other *impedimenta* of a major household move. My wife, Eileen, and I looked at each other and then answered, "No, why?"

"The story goes that Michael Collins actually stayed in this house for several nights, and the old doctor who owned it named it after him."

"Uh huh," we said, with furtive looks at each other, quietly hoping that the other knew who Michael Collins was.

"That was before he went on to get involved in that ghastly mess in Ireland."

Ah. That Michael Collins.

"This used to be his surgery. The doctor, of course, not Michael Collins," Stephanie went on. "He was so popular in the area during his prime that he had to build another home next door to release more rooms for the patients here."

I had visions of nurses rolling gurneys up and down the narrow halls in the bedroom area.

"With all these paneled walls and small turns, this doesn't seem like a place where I'd go to have an operation.

"Oh no," Stephanie giggled. "These were Mr. Valdinger's office and examining rooms. His surgery. Not a place to go to hospital."

"Whoa. I thought you said he was a doctor."

"Yes, and an excellent one."

"Then why do you call him Mr. Valdinger?"

Stephanie knit her face into a conspiratorial smile. "Well, you'll find that our medical professional has its own social strata. The everyday medical person that takes care of your warts and sniffles and the like is called Doctor. He can eventually graduate to Surgeon, or if he is somewhat gifted and mobile, to Professor. At the top of his trade, he reverts to the title Mister."

"As in Mister Valdinger."

"Righty–ho," she said as she touched my arm. "You understand."

I turned to Eileen. "How would you feel if the person poking his fingers around your aorta during a by-pass operation was named Mr. Jones?"

"Like a stewing chicken."

"Oh posh, you two," said Stephanie. "Anyway, I'll just give you the quick essentials of this place since you have all this horrid unpacking to do. I'll show you the rest in a few days. Have you mastered the cooker and hob?"

"Pardon me?" Eileen asked. "The cookeren knob?"

"Come along. I'll show you."

Stephanie led us to the kitchen stove, skirting ominous towers of cardboard dish boxes and a table covered with a lifetime's accumulation of cooking implements. "The hob operates off this dial," she showed as she turned on the oven. "The cooker off these," as she turned on the stovetop burners."

"Oh, right," Eileen allowed, bluffing her way through the moment. "The oven, er, hob only goes up to 250 degrees. It is just a warming oven?"

"That actually should be quite enough. You do know that's Celsius?"

"Oh yes. Celsius. My second favorite temperature scale. It's just that I can never remember if it's nine-fifths or five-ninths to get to the other one."

"The keys," Stephanie pressed on. "I'll have to show you those and the alarm system."

She presented us with a box filled with dozens of assorted keys. The front door key was a huge brass affair that looked like it would unlock the local cathedral. The back and side doors had their own separate keys. Each window, upstairs and down, had a tiny key. The garage had a key. The gardeners' commode at the side of the house had a key. The alarm system had a key and a code.

"It's quite distressing to need all these," Stephanie lamented. "I sometimes think we've become a nation of petty thieves and burglars. It hasn't been quite so bad since the economy improved. But still, you need to mind where you put things down. Someone will nick them in a moment.

"I'll pop back in a few days and see how you're coming along. All this unpacking would drive me to the end of my tether. Perhaps if you can clear way your kit enough to get to the front door, you could join Alistair and me and some of the neighbors from the close for a walk to the pub on Sunday."

"Super," I said, listening to how colonial my own words sounded. "I'm sure we can."

Eileen and I looked at each other. "I think I could get to like this place."

"Me too."

Here we were in Surrey, southwest of London. I had accepted an assignment with my company in Great Britain, after working thirty-four years in the States, twenty-nine of them in Houston, Texas. But I had tired of the sameness of the corporate life and searched for something else to do before I pulled the plug and retired. When an opportunity came up in the UK, I grabbed it and brought the news home.

After twenty-four hours in a glacially catatonic state, Eileen warmed to the idea of change and soon we embarked on a logistical maneuver of D-day proportions, moving out of the house we had lived in for twenty-six years.

In these days of corporate meanness, and I use the word in its every sense, companies expect their transferees to pack up whatever household goods they expect to need, fly off to their new assignment, find a house, and move in.

"That's the stupidest thing I ever heard of. How do we know what to bring?" Eileen wanted to know. After a week or so of ineffectively defending the Neanderthalian policy of our Human Resources Department, I saw the compelling logic of a house-hunting trip. I purchased two plane tickets out of my own pocket and made arrangements to stay with some old friends, Peter and Kelly, who had preceded us by eighteen months. Saturday night of Easter weekend we flew to London's Gatwick Airport.

"Right on time, sir. Just like Big Ben," said the ineffably cheery Brian, holding a sign that said "LEFFLER (2)." Kelly had hired a chauffeur and limo to pick us up at Gatwick. Any place in America, we would have rented a car for the forty-five mile trip to their house. But in the UK, everyone seems to hire drivers, judging by the blizzard of little white signs clustered around Brian.

"In from America, are you?"

"Yes," I said. "From Texas."

"Oh indeed? Lovely place, Texas. I visited Dallas and San Antonio. Rather hot this time of the year, right?"

Brian chatted incessantly the entire trip, giving us a complete tourist's portrait of Texas. I can't remember how many Brits we would meet just like Brian who knew as much about Texas as we did. Texas and Florida seemed to be perennial destinations for Brits. Every April to September, hordes of them, pale-faced and intrepid travelers, invade the American shores as if the War of 1812 had rolled around again. I suppose we win this time too.

"No time to sleep or unpack, darlings," said Kelly when we arrived. "You'll only waste precious time."

They loaded us in their estate wagon for a tour of Surrey, home to five thousand American ex-pats and London's biggest bedroom community. Up and down the borough we roamed - from their home in Oxshott to Leatherhead to Cobham to Epsom. We saw the train stations, the "best" shopping centers, and the favorite restaurants. Early spring is a wonderful time to house hunt. Yellow daffodils had burst from the fields and covered the roundabouts. In the roadside woods, tree branches bent heavy with buds. Flowers bordered the neat yards of every house we toured.

"No, no," Peter said to me when I offered these observations. "A yard is where one parks his lorry. The area around a house, especially in back, is a garden. Whether you're growing anything or not."

"And those are not woods," said Kelly. "It's the weald. Or a copse. And that scruffy open area down there with the daffodils is the heath."

"And I thought we spoke the same language," I said.

"Rahther provincial of you, dahling," gibed Kelly. "Any way, enough of this. It's already half-one. Let's off to eat. Why don't we try the Cricketer?" Which of course sounded fine to us.

On the fringe of Cobham, next to a large cricket pitch, hidden from the road by impenetrable hedgerows, sat a country pub. Of all the historic but declining institutions in this country, pubs tie with the monarchy as the most English. I'm convinced that without them, the depressingly long and drab winters with just seven hours of daylight filtered through rain and mist would have driven English emigration to Irish potato famine dimensions. Many public houses date back to medieval times, especially the country pubs. Clientele back then were more often travelers who could find no other means of sustenance or accommodation, and many pubs once doubled as inns. Alas now they offered only the essentials, food and drink.

"The Cricketer opened for business in the early 1700s," Peter told us as we stood in the car park. On this sunny Sunday, the light reflected off the white stucco walls and made the dark wooden beams look impressive. "It's amazing that the wattle and daub holds up as well as it does," he said.

"Waddling dodd?"

"No, no. Wattle and daub. They made the exterior walls by weaving tree branches in between the beams. Then they covered them with a plaster-like filler. You'd think after three or four centuries these you'd start to see some decay."

"I'd hate to see what our house in Houston would look like after three or four centuries. Or three or four decades. Or our kid's bedroom after three or four days."

"Mind your head," Kelly said, as we walked past the front door, a three-inch thick monster that swung wondrously with a push of the hand and closed with the resonance of a prison gate. Inside, the uneven ceilings were no more than 72 inches in most places. Some of the eight-by-twelve beams sagged here and there, making us stoop on the way to our table.

The focal point of most pubs is the bar, but at the Cricketer, my eye quickly went to the huge fireplace on a far wall. It was the only place tall enough to allow any of us to stand fearlessly upright. I shivered a moment as my mind's eye saw a bitter cold December night, a crackling fire of Yule logs, and mugs filled with Christmas cheer. Could this be a harbinger?

"The traditional pub fare for Sunday is the roast joint," Kelly told us. "A leg of mutton, a roast loin of pork, or a standing rib of beef. There, on the board.

They've got mutton today. Other things too. Come give your orders in at the window."

Waitstaff in a pub will deliver your meal (but not your drinks) and clear your table, but they don't take food orders. That works out well with the indigenous tipping habits. Unlike the profligate Americans who are embarrassed if anyone sees them drop less than 15 percent on a tab, a Brit will begrudgingly leave close to 10 percent – if someone is watching him. No doubt the institution of the public house has survived the centuries because they have eliminated tipping all together. Money changes hands at the order window or the bar. When the meal is over customers just get up and leave, unabashed and happy.

As an adventure in that oxymoron, British cuisine, I ordered the mutton. Gagging at the thought, Eileen ordered the chicken and sweet corn pie. The ladies found a table while Peter and I ordered drinks at the bar. An intimidating array of spouts presented themselves, each topped with colored medallions and logos.

"What'll the two of you have?" asked Peter.

"I suppose we better have a beer. Pick something out for us."

"We'll have two pints of Courage Best Bitter, and half pint of Tenant lager, and a lemonade, please," Peter asked of the barmaid, a brutally handsome lady with arms the size of ham hocks.

With her left hand she grabbed the long mahogany and ivory handle with the Courage emblem and gave a mighty pull. Her *carpi radialis* bulged with the strain as dark brown liquid flowed into the glass in her other hand. After a long stroke, she repeated the draw to fill the glass to overflowing. Before she started the second glass she put the smaller half-pint glass under the Tenant spout and flipped the handle with her finger. Amber brew started to flow into the glass. Both the bitter and the lager overflowed at the same time.

"What's that all about?" I asked her. "How come you have to struggle so much for one and not the other?"

"Wait till you taste the difference, luv," she said to me. "This one, the Tenant, has enough bubbles in it to pump itself out of the keg. That one I had to draw all the way from the cellar with my own hands."

Sure enough, the difference was clear. A hand-drawn pint is a wonderful thing. Freshness is everything in beer and this one probably had left the brewery no more than a day ago. Its temperature was cool, but not cold. It had a smooth, almost creamy texture. The low level of carbonation kept the bubbles from getting in the way of the flavor. Not that the colder, crisp Tenant lager would be all that bad on a hot day, but I decided right there I was a smooth and creamy, hand-drawn guy.

"I'll get it. How much is that?" I said to the barmaid.

"No, you can't," Peter told me and threw a ten pound note on the bar. Aside he said to me, "I'll tell you why when we get to the table."

Kelly's drink didn't look like lemonade to me. "Taste it'," she offered when we seated ourselves.

"It's Sprite. Or Seven-up," I said.

"Right. If you want lemonade, order lemon squash. And ask for ice, or you won't get it. They'll just pour a concentrate in the glass and then fill it with water, and that's lemonade."

"So back to why couldn't I pay. Did I embarrass myself without knowing it again?" I asked Peter.

"Almost. Whoever makes the first offer, the 'What'll you have?' he pays. No exceptions. You might insult someone by insisting."

Over the next hour Peter and I returned to the bar to practice "What'll you have?" so I'd get the hang of it. Three or four pints later, with stomachs full of bitter and lager and mutton and chicken and sweet corn, we left the Cricketer – without tipping. Eileen and I realized that we had only slept only two hours out of the last 36 and Sunday Roast had put us over the top. Blessedly, Peter and Kelly took us home and put us to bed.

The next two and half days, Nadia, our hired house-finder showed us 33 houses available for rent. After a dozen or so we began to give code names to the ones we wanted to remember. The Curry House had an Indian couple cooking in the kitchen. The Puke Green House had a nice floor plan but had to be repainted. The Highway House, The Roach House, the Slanty House, The Linoleum House, The Racetrack House … they all had something wrong.

In a stupor in the middle of the third day, I heard Nadia saying, "That's everything we have that fits your needs. I suppose you want to be as close to the community of American ex-pats as possible."

"Not really. We already know all the Americans we need to. We want a place where we can come to know the British. And we have only twelve months to do it."

"Well it's best then that you make an offer on one of the outliers. Even so, there's no guarantee you won't be gazumped by the time you're ready to move in."

"Gazumped. Did you make that word up?"

"No. Everyone in the business is always afraid of being gazumped – when someone overbids you before you have a chance to close on your house."

"Even if we have a contract on it? Is that legal?"

"Oh yes, unfortunately so. So I shouldn't bargain too hard on the price."

Oh blimey, I thought. What a country. I can't buy a fellow a two pound thirty lager if I don't follow the protocol but he can snatch my three hundred fifty thousand pound house from under my nose. Who are these people?

March 27

Dear Richard,

Well, we're here and we're in. The movers finally delivered our stuff, even though the sign on the side of their van – or rather lorry – said "Removals."

Anyway, while we waited for the shipment to hit the shores, and I think that might have been what happened, we shopped for some essentials that we couldn't bring with us, like a small electric kettle that Kelly tells me is absolutely necessary here. Good thing too. The so-called decorators were working to get the house ready for us. When we stopped in, we were disappointed to meet them – two painters in white overalls and painters' caps on backwards. One had a shaved head, four earrings, and an ugly purple bruise on his lip. And he was the supervisor. The other one had half-closed eye and a limp. They were a pleasant enough pair, however. When I offered them a cup of tea, they started falling all over themselves with excitement. "Oh that would be just lovely," they bubbled. And these were grown men that looked like they bash heads at the pub for sport on weekends.

I noticed their enthusiasm ebbed a little when I got out the Earl Grey tea bags. I finally got them to tell me that NO ONE drinks Earl Grey anymore and that they would prefer P.G. Tips the next time. Well excuuse me.

I called over to the local satellite television agent to have the system in our house hooked up. The friendly lady told me that Mr. Seabridge, the engineer, would be able to come over on Friday morning and that he prefers coffee to tea. I even had her repeat it. Then Mr. Chesterton, the furniture restorer, came on Thursday afternoon to assess the damage to our dining room set and other pieces. During tea, he used up all the milk for Mr. Seabridge's coffee. It didn't matter though, because on Friday morning our American coffeemaker blew out and Mr. Seabridge didn't get anything at all.

I had a mental lapse last week. I parked the car in the front driveway, inside the gates, mind you, and left my purse in the front seat while I ran into the house to check the mail. When I came out five minutes later, the purse was gone. I'm sure it was those worthless decorators who were constantly in and out at the time, but I can't prove it. Well, no more P. G. Tips for them. Constable Woosely has been assigned the case and he called and told me he'd "pop in" on Wednesday to get the details. I wonder if he drinks tea or coffee.

Your loving (and coping) sister, Eileen

Bill Leffler

2

Bees

The sun warmed the new growth of the lawn. The crocus had already come and gone and the daffodils had poked their yellow heads above beds of sweet william and sage. The plum trees had donned their bright purple coats. The bees busied themselves about the apple blossoms, doing their magic to set the fruit…

The bees! Oh no, it was bee season, and an insect sting will make my extremities swell like the *Graf Zepelin* while my face turns an ugly shade of purple. None of the windows in our newly leased house had any screens, so Eileen and I faced a dilemma. We could close the windows, keep out the bees, and swelter or open them and risk having me inflate and float off in the fresh springtime breezes.

Unhappy with those options, we decided we needed screens, even if at our own expense. Friday morning, Eileen stopped at the Ironmonger in Cobham and asked the proprietor where we might get either screens or screen material to make some. "Screens?" he said, shaking his head. "Do you mean like the Japanese put in their rooms?"

"No, no. Screens. Like to keep the bugs out of our house."

"To do what?"

"To keep the insects from flying in the open windows."

" 'Fraid I can't help you, madam."

Eileen concluded this might be harder than we guessed.

Saturday morning I decided the Yellow Pages would solve our problem. I found two ads for window companies who offered season-end prices all year for installation of double-glazing, which I took to mean storm windows. I called. The first number rang fifteen times with no response. The second got an answering machine that informed me the office didn't open until nine (it was then 10:30) and that I should call back tomorrow (which would be Sunday.)

Only moderately daunted, Eileen and I started out. We visited the ironmonger in Hersham, well known for his fix-it knowledge. "Screens?" he said. "I have some metal mesh, but I'm afraid it won't keep out the small insects. It's meant to detain rabbits and chickens and the like. Have you tried the Cobham Ironmonger?"

On exit, I spotted a shop directly across the street advertising "window systems."

"The solution is at hand," I announced to Eileen. Together we entered and inquired of the salesperson. He began the same doleful head wagging of the ironmongers. We wondered whether it was a local affliction. "Window screens? Well, I'm not quite sure. Hang on."

"Ian. Ian," he yelled towards the back office. "Do you know anything about window screens?"

"What's that? You mean like on a car? A windscreen?" returned a voice from the unseen Ian. I half-yelled back my interpretation of a window system – how it might include screens that are seasonally interchangeable with the double-glazed windows.

"I'm afraid I can't help you. You might try the Homebase in Walton-on-Thames. Very modern store. They have everything there."

We left the disembodied Ian and his salesperson pondering the true meaning of "window systems" and drove to Walton-on-Thames. Homebase, an English attempt at Home Depot, appeared to be more floor space than merchandise. Ten-foot wide aisles were bounded with five-foot high shelving. It was not a good omen to see nuts and bolts tastefully, but sparsely, set out in rows on the shelves. With more somber head shaking, the store manager suggested that the person who might know how to solve our problem was Porter, the local glazier, and he was only a few blocks away.

"Through the alley, across the verge, then down the lane and straight-away. You can't miss him."

Sure.

After three alleys, two lanes, and four enquiries, we found the glazier in a tiny Dickensian shop, curiously devoid of windows. The skeptical Porter rejected the whole notion that English homes needed any covering for their windows. "No insects to speak of, really. And bees are seldom interested in entering dark places."

"We had three of them in our house just yesterday," I offered in evidence.

Baffled by the whole concept, Porter suggested we might "nip in" to the locksmith's, further down the lane. He sometimes installed security systems on windows and might have an idea. I could hear him mumbling something about "Americans" as we left.

The distinct odor of solvents and lubricating oil led us to the locksmith's shop. Hunched over a workbench was an unshaven and tattooed hulk, with rings in his ears and a large chip missing from a front tooth. He brushed away the machine parts in front of him and rested his chin on his oily hand as we explained our mission. "'At's a good one, mate," he said with a little whistle through the gap in his incisors. "Hain't never been asked 'at before. Fiona. 'Ear whot these people want? Something to keep the bees out of their home. Got any ideas?"

"Maybe lace curtains," came a tiny voice from the back. We looked up to see that Fiona had materialized behind the locksmith. She looked like a waif of no more than fourteen years, but she was at least eight months pregnant. The frightened look on her face made me think she had just witnessed a beheading or something equally ghastly. Maybe she was married to the locksmith and was thinking about having to spend the rest of her life with him.

"'Air you go, mates. Lace curtains. Won't keep out much else, but it'll keep out them bees." The locksmith thought this was the funniest security joke he had ever cracked and was still bowled over with laughter as we backed out of the shop thanking him for his advice. Fiona had slipped back into the shadows.

"Lace curtains all over our house," said Eileen. "I don't think so. And who would buy even a key from that guy, no less a security system? He looks like an extra from a Mad Max movie."

By the time we arrived home, we had started to wag *our* heads. We were concluding we would have to wait until our next trip to America when we could buy the materials and make our own screens. Then Eileen thought of the handyman who worked for our landlord.

I called him and asked, "Colin, what should we do to keep the bees from coming in our open windows?" Maybe a new way to ask the question would help.

"How about lace curtains?"

"No, we've already been through that with someone else."

In another moment Colin suggested, "You might do what I did for my caravan. I went to the accessories store in Leatherhead and bought some fly screen. That might work. His shop is right on the Leatherhead Roundabout."

"Uhhh, caravan?"

"Yes, what you Yanks call travel trailers. Caravans. We use fly screen to keep out the mosquitoes when we camp in the weald."

"Ah, perfect." I said. "And do you know where I might buy some thin wood stripping to make some frames?"

"You'll want beading. That's what they call it here. Beading." Colin is very patient with Americans. "Try any DIY store," he said.

"Uhhh, DIY?"

"Do It Yourself," Colin said.

Sure enough, when Eileen looked in the Yellow Pages, she found a category called "DIY."

One more trip, this time to Leatherhead, and Eileen and I came home with packages of one and two-meter squares of nylon screen, nearly the same gauge as the real thing. In an hour, a few strategically placed Velcro strips let us cover a half dozen windows but still work the latches, locks, and cranks to open the swing-outs.

The air is warm. The wisteria sways in the breeze. The bees busily move from blossom to blossom, collecting nectar and dispersing pollen. But they are unable to assault the dark place where we now lounge, coolly, securely, now *nodding* our heads smugly.

April 21

Dear Richard,

Contrary to popular belief, some of the food in this country is really good. Especially the baked goods. I went down to the bakery in the little town of Claygate this morning and they were selling Hot Cross Buns in celebration of Easter. I never knew that was where the name came from. Our mouths just water for their scones, but they were already all out, at ten in the morning.

We pumped up our courage and put invitations in the mailboxes of all the neighbors in the close for a Texas Gumbo party. I'm sure they had no idea what gumbo was, but they all responded and fourteen of them came Sunday night. Every one of them brought something, a bottle of wine, box of candy, or flowers. We served salad and chicken-andouille gumbo. Good thing we had plenty of both because four of them were vegetarians and had to fill up on bread and greens.

After everyone was seated, I walked into the dining room to find them all sitting quietly looking at their salad, but not eating. I encouraged them to start and one guest demurely asked if they could have knives. I hadn't put them out because there was nothing to cut and I had already lathered the bread with garlic butter. But we found out that Brits don't eat anything unless they have a knife to push it on to their fork.

Today I found an envelope in the mail basket marked "By hand." It was the first of seven thank you notes and in this one the lady remarked, "… and your Jumbo was lovely."

21

I miss Target and K-Mart. Can you believe I'd ever say that? Finding all the little things like shower curtain hooks is a hassle since the supermarkets don't sell anything but food. And even then ... I went to Waitrose Market yesterday to get some brownie mix and finally had to ask the manager where the cake mix section was. He took me over to aisle 2 and showed me. There was a chocolate cake mix and a vanilla cake mix. That was it. We had ice cream for dessert last night.

While at the market I tried to push my basket up to the counter marked "baskets only" but the aisle was too narrow. And I had been wondering why the ladies behind me were glaring. "Won't fit'," I appealed to the checker. "Sorry mum, but this line is for baskets only," she sniffed. "We take our trolleys to those other counters."

We joined a tennis club about ten miles away and the pro has arranged my first game tomorrow. He didn't seem too familiar with what a 4.5 ranking is. I'm a little nervous anyway because I'm probably rusty after not playing for three months now.

Love, your homesick sister

3

Doone

In the center of Glastonbury, amidst the Abbey ruins, lays a 6 by 10 plot of trimmed grass. A sign announced it to be the site of the former burial place of King Arthur and Lady Guinevere. Now, movies with Richard Gere and Sean Connery aside, King Arthur is a legend. The scholars agree. Even the Glastonbury Tourist Center pamphlets talk about the legend in mystical terms, using the words "believed by some," and "supposedly." Yet the Glastonbury Abbey elders still assert that they have found the royal grave site, coincidentally right in the middle of their Abbey (Admission: £2.50)

The British have a way of blurring history with fiction. In this town in Devon, at the base of the stump that makes up southwestern England, the frantic pace of London and its suburbs gives way to farm communities of unchanging serenity and conservatism. Yet in incomprehensible bursts of regress, they exploit the alleged past with shameless intensity.

"Most everyone believes some of it," the Abbey duty officer told us. "That's why we have all these mystic shops about."

It was true. At breakfast one Saturday morning in the Spiral Gate Organic Café, we were jarred by the aromatic smell of incense mixed with aroma of fresh baked scones. High Street was replete with shop widows filled with Tarot cards, sorcerer's capes, brass dragons, and magic potions. On one corner we heard sitar music, and another New World guitar.

"'At's why all those teens come here in the summer. For the Glastonbury Festival. It rains every year and they smoke those funny cigarettes and roll in the mud and do Lord knows what else," the guard had said with a trace of envy. "Then they chant all that weird hocus pocus about witches and covens and such. Creepy, if you ask me."

Further down the coast in Cornwall, the folks of Tintagel have taken the Arthur legend to exasperatingly commercial absurdity. On our way through the town, we passed a sign advertising the Excali-Bar in King Arthur's Hotel, home of Excali-beer. We chose not to have lunch in Arty's restaurant, Arturo's Italian Fayre, or Guinivere's Tea Shoppe. The imaginative owners of Lancelot's Inn had two large plastic dragons at their entrance that threatened passing tourists to enter at their own risk.

We stopped at the tiny interpretive center at Titagel Castle to explore the myth some more. The castle ruins sit atop a prominence, guarding the entrance to a small, treacherously rocky harbor off the Atlantic. A squall had just blown in. The rain slapping against the windowpanes reminded us why we were the only tourists there that day.

"Can I show you our history?" boomed the docent, a burly lady. The crossbar of the white cross blazoned on her red Arthurian doublet was folded under a huge bosom and almost hidden. "We've just had a wonderful discovery."

Always game to hear more, we offered our encouragement.

"We had some of those archaeologists from the University of Glasgow here and they found this plaque." She showed us a picture of a piece of grey slate with some scratching on it. A label underneath interpreted the inscription to say *pater coliavificit Artognov.*

"It means, 'Arthnou, father of a descendent of Coll, had this place built.'" I wondered why someone would be called father of a descendent.

"Where did they find it?" Eileen asked her.

"Under a pile of shale in the castle ruins. We know for sure that Arthnou was an intrepid chieftain that fought a dozen battles against invaders in the twelfth century. It's almost certain proof that this was the castle where Arthur held his meetings with the Knights of the Round Table. We've found their things about the castle site. "

"You mean, like, they left their brollies in the closet?" I said in an unchivalrous moment. Daggers shot out of Eileen's eyes.

"No, dear," said our stout instructress without falter. "Cutlery, crockery, shoe buckles, the artifacts of 12th century wealth."

By then the rain had settled into a Cornwall mist – too still to call it drizzle, too wet to call it fog. We decided to wander through the ruins and look for more shoe buckles. We could hear the waves relentlessly pounding the rocky coastline, even over our puffing as we climbed the steep stone and wooden stairway to the keep. Wealth and majesty now left scant evidence behind among the foundations and remaining half-walls of the castle.

"Do you suppose one of these rooms is a bedroom?" I asked Eileen.

"Nah. I'm sure nobility would want an ocean view. Let's look over there."

Alas, 20 minutes of random poking yielded no relics of Artognov or his knights, so we returned to our car as the cold mist set our teeth chattering. "Come milady," I said. "Let us take ourselves from this sodden citadel to yon publick house for a warming cup of tea."

"Aye, my prince," said the fair maid, Eileen, "but methinks a flagon of mead would suit me better."

Later that day we came to Porlock, a town in the midst of Lorna Doone country in the County of Devon. We had never read R. D. Blackstone's 1868 novel about Lorna Doone, so we were pleased to find a three-page synopsis in the sitting room of our Bed & Breakfast. It read like *Romeo and Juliet on the Moors*. We were glad we hadn't tried the 400-page version.

The story, the B&B summary said, is set in a loosely documented historical background involving the Doone family, a notorious clan of brigands living in the valley south of Porlock. Blackstone's success as an author seemed to have been the most notable thing that happened to the area in the last 150 years and North Devon had jumped on the Lorna Doone bandwagon. Porlock has a Lorna Doone Hotel, a Doone Restaurant, and the Lorna Doone Tea Shoppe. Eight miles outside of town was the Lorna Doone Trail.

"You must walk the trail," insisted Neville, our B&B host, at breakfast. "Lovely this time of year and a delightful amble amongst the hills."

Indeed, yellow sunshine poured into the breakfast nook, bouncing off the silverware and plates. On the shrubs outside the window, dewdrops from last night's mist reflected a beautiful day. We could almost hear Ms. Doone herself beckoning us. So off we went, trail guide in hand, to hike.

Reaching the trailhead in the village of Malmstead became a challenge in itself. Devon must have the narrowest roads in England. Neville had explained the hierarchy of byways in Britain. "Roads connect the towns. Streets are the passageways in the towns. Lanes are where the cottages are."

Still we were used to finding, at least on the roads, that the pavement abuts a shoulder. That could be a few feet of concrete, asphalt, grass, or maybe just dirt. But in the Devon lowlands, the pavement ended abruptly at a tall, lush hedge, growing to heights of 8-15 feet. What seemed so, well, British, was the care with which the hedgerows had been treated. In most of what we saw in Devon, a highway crew had been recently by with a vertical blade and trimmed the hedgerow back a half foot. The swath they had cut reached from ground level to about 6 feet. Above that, the leafy growth reached randomly over the road.

On the road from Porlock, these hedgerow tunnels left our dark blue and dusty estate wagon with horizontal stripes on the left side every time we passed a car from the opposite direction. When buses approached, we cowered in the vegetation until they passed.

Our guidebook took us from the valley up 2000 feet to the top of Porlock Hill. Even with the remnants of a hazy mist over the Bristol Channel, we could see Wales across the way, dense with primeval forest. As we rounded a sharp curve near the top, Eileen screeched. A half dozen sheep lolled on the roadway. The roads on the hilltops not only had no hedgerows, they had no fences at all, allowing the sheep to range up and down the hillside in search of a late breakfast.

"Look there," Eileen said. Ten yards beyond the lounging sheep stood a yellow highway sign with the black silhouette of a sheep. "Now they tell us."

Atop Porlock Hill, we found a hut-size structure, attended by a hardy lady who cheerfully gave us hiking advice, and sold us another guide booklet. "This one by the Friends of Lorna Doone is much better. It gives you two choices. You can start from here and hike down the valley to Malmstead, then follow the Doone trail. Or you can drive down to Malmstead and they'll start you from there."

"Who are 'they'?" I asked.

"Oh, I'm sure there'll be some one to help."

We went out to the edge of the small car park and gazed down into the valley on the backside of Porlock Hill. For a moment I fanaticized about a childhood pastime – starting a grapefruit-sized snowball at the top of a hill, seeing how large it could get before it reached the bottom. With a 2000 foot run, I imagined the *Porlock News* headline, "Avalanche wreaks foot-wide path of destruction through village."

Without a word Eileen and I both turned back to the car to drive the first leg. At the top of the single-track road down to the valley a sign warned,

CAUTION 1:2 SLOPE

Eileen, the trigonometrix of our family, quickly calculated we were on a 30-degree decline, with no traversing. "It's the '1, 2, square root of 3 'rule." I was sure she was right as the smell of brake lining wafted through the car vents.

The deeper into the valley we drove, the more frequently we uttered, "Oh thank you God for saving me from that walk back up the hill."

By now we were on what British Automobile Association referred to as unclassified roads. We were off the maps and totally reliant on Lorna's friends and their guidebook. At the bottom of the valley, we came to a small river crossing and what the friends noted was a 17th century packhorse bridge over Badgworthy Water, the border between Somerset and Devon. The Royal Commission for Old Things or some such office had declared it an Ancient Monument, putting it in the Stonehenge category. The bridge looked so narrow we weren't sure we could get all four tires on it at one time. The alternative seemed to be fording the river, the preferred choice of some earlier vehicles, based on the tracks on the bank. With visions of our car filling with water as the tires spun in the silt, I opted for the bridge.

"I'll guide you," said Eileen, jumping out of the car. It occurred to me that she had the safer of the two jobs.

As I eased the front wheels onto the short but steep bridge, the front end pointed so high I could only see the grimace on her face over the hood as I drifted too

31

close to one edge or the other. Meter by meter she gave me expressive, if not express, guidance across.

We were four or five miles beyond when we were happy to see a robust hiking family coming at a brisk pace toward us. We stopped them and asked if we were on the right route to Malmstead.

"Straight-away," they advised us, which was lucky, because we saw little opportunity to make a U-turn, having returned to the endless hedgerows of the lowlands.

I wondered what we were supposed to do when we met a vehicle coming in the opposite direction. On this single-track road, allegedly to Malmstead, we could literally reach out both side windows and touch greenery. On encounter, one of us would have to back up and find a driveway, or cow path or a crossroad. On the long stretches where none of those were available, the road engineers had strategically placed a wide spot in the road about every 300 yards.

I never did hear what the rules of engagement were on these hedgerow passageways. Mostly our estate wagon intimidated our opponents and they sullenly gave way or backed up. Where discretion bested valor, usually involving an encounter with a Land Rover, I retreated up the lush tunnel to the closest lay-by where they would pass us, always with a wave of the hands and a wan smile.

At last we arrived at Malmstead. We knew because one of the four stone buildings had a sign that announced "Malmstead Gifts." A car park with four vehicles offered the only other signs of human endeavour. This was what a hamlet must look like. We crossed another narrow stone bridge over another small river (or maybe the same one), reverting to our creep and blanch technique.

On our tailgate in the car park, we enthusiastically donned our hiking boots and then took several false starts until we realized we had no idea which way to head. The guidebook was totally indecipherable.

"Can I help you?" said an amiable Devonshire accented voice. He was dressed in the tweed of a country squire, brown shirt and browner tie, feet firmly planted in Wellies, the ubiquitous calf-high rubber boots of the countryside. On one shoulder rested a flyrod; from the other hung a wicker creel.

"You'll want to backtrack a little, turn left onto the cow path and go past Parsonage Farm. Real farm, eh? Modern buildings and all. Straight away along the river till you get to the Oare House and the Oare Church. Then up to the moors. The path gets a little dodgey after that, eh? But look for the tearoom where you'll want to stop for a cup of tea. Don't come back by the road from there, eh? You'll want to take this trail back here," as he pointed to our guidebook.

Off we went to find our cowpath, and for the next two hours we never knew quite where we were. We walked along the farm and both buildings did indeed look like they had been built within the last century. The path along the river surrounded us with lush green – the trees and especially the grass. This was not the hard green of summer, nor the dusty green of fall. It was the intense green of promise and renewal, ripe with the smell of chlorophyll.

Sheep and new lambs milled out of our way, bleating their disapproval. Gnats swarmed frenetically over the river, but kept to themselves. We passed the same hiking family again, mother and father, 6 and 8 year olds, and got confirmation we were still on the right track. "I know," I said. "Straight-away."

"Right," they said, grinning.

The jewel in the crown of Doone Country is Oare Church. By itself on a knoll, it seemed the only reason why two roads would intersect at his spot. The stone building was no more than 70 feet long and 30 feet wide. As we walked up, we saw a sign leaning against the entrance arch. "Visitors may wait until this morning's service is ended or join us."

With that ambivalent invitation, we poked our heads around the heavy wooden door to see the clergyman and his congregation gathered in the back of the church. "May we come in?" I whispered to one of them.

Someone responded, "But of course. Do join us."

Other faces and voices, but not the vicar's, joined in, enthusiastically bidding us to enter. We surmised the reason in a few moments. The whole congregation consisted of six people, two of whom turned out to be the sexton and his wife. All were in their seventies or more. They seemed happy to see more people join the group. The vicar nodded with a furrowed brow as we introduced ourselves.

"Won't you join us for coffee and biscuits?" the sexton's wife asked.

How could we refuse? Even though I'm allergic to caffeine, it seemed out of the question to ask for de-caf.

Where were we from? What were we doing here? How did we like living in England? In a few moments the coffee and cookies arrived. "You must try some of the biscuits. Mrs. Dilworthy makes them herself."

We should have guessed. In the middle of the tray lay a dozen cookies – Lorna Doones – presenting us one of those incomparable moments of congruity – the place, the people, the mood, and the cookies, er, the biscuits.

"I visited my son in Houston last year," the sexton said. "People there thought he was loony, you know. He lived in one of those condominium places, about a mile from work. He'd walk to and from work every day. They couldn't believe he wouldn't drive.

"Houston was the hottest place I've ever been. Wouldn't ever want to go back. Ever," he said, shaking his head and shuffling off to his duties at the altar.

We wandered about the small church and saw a slit of a window along the south side of the nave, just as the guidebook predicted. A tiny sign resting on the sill proclaimed,

"This is the window through which Lorna Doone was shot by Carver Doone, according to R. D. Blackmore." There was no mention of the words "novel" or "fiction," just unqualified fact. With a hint of ecclesiastic irony, another plaque further down the nave told us that R. D. Backmore's grandfather was rector of this church from 1809-42.

The vicar had left without a word to us. I supposed I'd be a little disheartened and even grumpy if my parish numbered only a half dozen plus an occasional stray tourist. During our good-byes to the others, I suggested to the sexton that he come visit Texas again.

"Not on your life! Terrible place."

Outside, our guidebook directed us "to carry on, up through the steep pastures beyond the church." It assured us that there would be "waymarks as guides around the head of a coombe, past the sheep pens and on to a field gate."

We had never seen the head of a coombe before or even knew what a coombe or a waymark were, so we trudged along a deep ravine, up the fields, through nervous sheep in one, bored cows in the next.

"Aha," Eileen said as we neared the top of the hill. A tiny sign nailed to a fencepost had the words, "hiking path" and an arrow pointing past the end of the ravine. "A waymark and the head of a coombe."

With unfailing accuracy, the arrow pointed us to the pens and a rusty gate through a fence. We were now at a crest, with Porlock Hill to our right, a deep the valley in between. Impossibly verdant pastures struggled up equally high hills to our front and left. The sheep grazing on the distant slopes were sprinkled like dandruff on a green blazer.

In a few more paces we happened upon a couple, probably in their late seventies, who had spread out a picnic for themselves at this beautiful spot. A wicker basket, little dishes of salads and meats, silverware, and a thermos, undoubtedly full of hot tea, covered their plaid blanket. With him in his tweeds and her in her flowered cotton dress and sensible shoes, we expected a romantic story. Perhaps this was the spot where he had proposed 50 years ago. Maybe it was their favorite vista, where they come to hold hands and enjoy the scenery.

"Actually," the old gentlemen said, as he made gurgling sounds with his pipe, "first time we've been here. We got lost about an hour ago, but we're so hungry, we decided to stop and eat. Seemed as good a place as any. They keep the sheep out of this meadow so there's no flop."

How entirely deflating.

With renewed confidence in our guidebook, we marched down the hill to Cloud Farm, a collection of stables and farm buildings. In the midst we found a small clapboard cottage with a hand painted sign, "Teahouse."

Outside, a dozen people sat at tables covered with pots and cups and plates piled with scones. Some people scooped gobs of Devonshire clotted cream and strawberry jam on to split scones. Others busied themselves with a proper tea. Those who had already finished their first pot poured hot water from the second into the first to wring the remaining bit of flavor from the once through teabags. Copious amounts of sugar and cream completed the finished product. We listened closely, expecting to hear their hearts pounding like a smithy's hammer and their plaque-laden veins sucking like a straw in an empty milk shake. Instead, amid quiet symphony of clinking cutlery on china and a soft patter of contentment, the only distinct word we heard was "lovely."

While Eileen had her tea and I my lemon squash, a half dozen horse riders splashed through a nearby stream and bounded up the hill past us to the stables.

"Well yes, we do have a few spots left that you could book," said the tea lady, when I asked. "There's a ride out to the moors at three. Nine quid."

I signed us up and went back to finish our teatime delights.

The moors. To me the word brought visions of Daphne DuMaurier's Rebecca, running from the manor house, across foggy marshland, fear in her eyes.

"What are the moors, anyway?" I asked Eileen.

"I was hoping you knew."

At three, a redheaded teenager, Katie, held our horses ready. "Would you please help yourselves to the proper headgear from the equipment room?"

Eileen and I dutifully traded our baseball caps for riding helmets. These were not quite the darling black velvet headgear with a button on top that we had seen competitive jumpers wear. They were more like black melon rinds made of polypropylene. With some searching we found two that we could get on our heads and still get the straps linked under our chins. Feeling haughty in our proper costume, we marched out to mount up.

"Sorry," said Katie. "You might want to put the part of the hat with insignia in the front."

So much for our sartorial prowess.

I can't remember a time when we have gone horseback riding when we didn't get animals of exactly the same personality as these. My horse, a ton of rippling, coal black muscle and bone named Charger, stood so tall, I could not see over his saddle. I had to stand ignominiously on a stool to get a foot in the stirrup. I didn't let on to Katie I was from Texas.

As soon as I mounted, Charger and I communicated without speaking, I thought. I knew he didn't want to be on this ride. He knew I knew he didn't. We understood each other perfectly. Charger would drag himself out on the first half of the ride. Exactly at midpoint, he would suddenly become enervated and head back towards the barn at an indefatigable pace. If I cared to join him, I would have to direct my full attention to staying atop.

Eileen's horse, Muffie, on the other hand, clearly had not eaten for three weeks. Every 25 yards she would stop, bend down and chew on the grass, drink out of a stream, or make a meal out of the tree leaves along the trail. Katie would have to come back and whack her on the butt – Muffie's, not Eileen's – with her crop to keep us moving.

I call it the Equine Conspiracy, and have learned to live with it.

Katie led us across and along the burbling stream, through a canopied forest, and turned up a steep hill. She announced, "This will get us to the moors."

The mystery started to unwind. We were heading up to the highlands, not down to the sea. In a short while we were beyond the tree line, plodding past meter high, purple-tinged vegetation.

"Heather?" I asked Katie.

She wagged her head. "Gorse."

"What's the difference between the two?" Eileen persisted

"You wouldn't want to fall off your horse into a bed of gorse. Rather all spiny and prickly. Heather's softer. Both purple."

"What's the dark stuff over there?"

"Rather awful, isn't it? It's bracken. It has almost no color and adds nothing to the brae. But it's starting to overtake the gorse on some slopes. A tragedy, really."

As we reached the first crest, we came to a tumble of barren hills rolling out to the horizon. With the sun behind a cloud, for the moment the bleak landscape offered not a hint of hospitality. Yet in a few moments as the sun reappeared, the slightest breeze turned the hills to wonderfully shimmering waves on a purple ocean.

"Now tell me, what exactly are the moors," Eileen asked.

"Well, they're rather like the top of a small mountain range. The Crown has owned them for centuries. They stretch from Bristol Bay on the north all they way down the Exmoor and into the Dartmoor, almost to the Channel. No one grazes them, I suppose because they're mostly covered with the gorse and bracken."

Apparently Muffie was unaware of contemporary tastes because she continued to reach down incessantly to bite off more late lunch.

Atop another hill we wandered past an area clear of vegetation. In the center stood two barrel-sized stones. Around the perimeter smaller stones formed a circle. Two shaggy horses, no taller than my chest, lounged in the circle.

"We have a treat for you," exclaimed Katie. "The wild ponies are ever so shy and we usually only see them across the valleys amongst the gorse."

"But what is that corral they're in?" I asked.

"Oh it has rather nothing to do with the ponies. It's a prehistoric altar. Distant kin to Stonehenge, I would suppose. The local coven gathers here once a year for some of their strange ceremonies. They say they do ritual sacrifices and raise spirits of old town folk.

"Have you ever watched?"

"Rather unlikely. My mum wouldn't let me do something like that."

We continued our gentle ride, rising and falling with the moorscape, until Katie told us we would take one last sweep. With hardly a warning, she kicked her horse to a gallop. Charger took this cue as the critical halfway mark and rose to the occasion. Gorse, and I suppose bracken, exploded around me, sticking to my clothes and hair as Charger's eyes blazed with the full knowledge that the faster he ran, the sooner his Valhalla, the stable, would loom up in front of him. I held on with legs and hands, contributing absolutely nothing to direction or the rate of speed.

Down the hill, through the woods, and into the stream we rocketed, amid splashing mud and water. Behind me I could see no sign of Katie or Eileen. I had visions of them beating Muffie with a stick to wean her away from the gorse-snacks. For fifteen minutes Charger bounded in and out of the stream. I hoped he knew the way because I had long since dropped the reins when we vaulted over a fallen log, thinking that holding on to the saddle would do more for me than flimsy leather straps. And why don't the English have horns on their saddles anyway?

Over a knoll we abruptly came upon Cloud Farm and Charger decelerated so quickly I almost flipped over his head. He trotted up to the stables and stopped to drink from the water trough. We waited another ten minutes before Eileen and Katie appeared. Eileen started laughing as they approached.

"What's so funny?" I asked her.

"You look like a purple topiary," she said.

I looked at myself and saw vegetation cemented with mud on major parts of my body, from helmet to sneaker. Muffie eyed me ravenously.

"Time to finish our walk to Malmstead," I said as I slid down to the ground with some effort and pain.

We still had a mile to walk to get back to our car in Malmstead, fortunately almost all downhill. About halfway, we stumbled upon a worn stone building set in a leafy glen, back from the road. The swaying sign hanging in front announced

The Blackguard
A Freehouse

What luck. We had found our own Valhalla.

"Uh-oh," I said, glancing at my watch. "I wonder if this pub closes from two to six."

It is only in the last few years that Parliament, trying to shed its nanny image, had removed yet another of its many restrictions. This one used to require pubs to close during the afternoon when working men shouldn't be tempted by the pint. Some privately owned pubs still kept to this strict schedule and closed their doors at two.

"Let's try," said Eileen, pushing open the door. The dark interior was quiet and empty except for an aproned bartender reading a newspaper at the bar. "Closed till six," he said.

"No exceptions for a couple of bedraggled travelers?" I pleaded.

The publican took a double take at me. "My lord, man. What happened to you? Have they dragged you through the bloody hedgerows?"

"I could tell the story a lot better over a pint of bitter," I offered.

"Well, I think we might be able to accommodate that," said our newfound friend, and he drew back the long handle with the Strong's Bitter logo and pumped the dark brew into a pair of glasses. "Roddy Blackmore," he said as he extended his hand over the two pints he placed on the bar. We introduced ourselves.

"Blackmore," I conjectured. "You must be related to the author,"

"Right you are. A great-great-uncle. And a great writer, I hear." Roddy said.

Over his head and dominating the room was a huge painting of a strikingly familiar black horse. Roddy noticed my fixation with it, which was probably not hard, what with my mouth agape and suds foaming on my upper lip.

"Beautiful piece of horse flesh, isn't he?" Roddy said. Without a hint of improbability in his voice he went on. "Originally owned by Carver Doone. That horse was a legendary sire about here. They even have one of his direct descendants at Cloud Farm."

Then his eyes began to widen as he resurveyed my disheveled and foliaged appearance. "Say, mate," he said. "You wouldn't happen just to have been riding the Doone Trail on a black horse named Charger, now would you?"

May 12

Dear Richard,

They certainly don't make it very easy to get a driver's license here. First I had to send in an application with a £10 fee. Then I bought the instruction books for £10. I've already taken the written test (£15) that I think I passed after reading the manuals a few times. Now I have to take the driving test (£25). All the other Americans here told me I needed to take driving lessons from Mr. Goodpasture so I signed up for three, at £16 a pop. And I can see why. The "proper" techniques are arcane. You have to put on the emergency brake every time you go from forward to reverse or even just stop. So to make a three point U-turn you have to stop, look in all three mirrors, put the brake on, shift, look in the mirrors, take the brake off, move, put the brake on, look in the mirrors, shift, take the brake off... and on and on. And this is in an automatic transmission car!

Mr. Goodpasture is supposed to come with me for the test (another £16), so I'm into this thing for £124 and I don't even have my license yet.

I went over to Claygate yesterday and they were out of scones again – at 9:30 this time. I asked the lady how come they're always out and why they don't make more. "Well actually, we seem to have the right number each day because they all get sold."

I couldn't bring myself to argue with that logic.

I've been assigned to the D Team at the tennis club. I can never tell that to my old tennis team in Houston, the ones I went with to Palm Springs and won the 4.5 Nationals. They'll think that D is for "Disgrace."

But my young partner and the team captain, Lulu (and she is one), assured me that the letter has nothing to do with the level. Still, neither she nor I can ever get a game with any of the A Team. They seem to be a pretty smug, tight clique.

They Just Don't Get It: The other evening we needed a bottle of Scotch whiskey and Bill wasn't sure the liquor store would be open. So he looked in the Yellow Pages under L. No luck. Then he looked under W for wine. Then S for spirits. Exasperated, he started with the A's and flipped pages until he found it under O. You know. O for Off-License – Wine and Spirits. Of course.

Love, your grappling sister

4

Battles

In the late 1600's, His Majesty's Cartographer, John Ogleby, created the earliest known road maps of Britain. The way from London to Portsmouth was among his first. He laid out his routes on a long ribbon-like design – down the page, folded under and up, then down and up the page four more times. Along the way he showed the cities, towns, a hamlet or two, and sketches of notable landmarks. It was as an AAA trip-tick might have looked in the seventeenth century.

We especially liked this map because the London to Portsmouth road passes only 300 yards from Michael Court. Ogleby penned in the old Esher Church, the one in which we just attended their semi-annual services just as Queen Victoria did a hundred and twenty years ago. We don't know why Ogleby didn't include the Bear, the coaching inn that casts its shadow on little Esher Church. Our Esher history books told us the Bear has been in continuous service since a hundred years before Ogleby's mapping. In its prime, it provided accommodations to travelers on the second night of the trip from Normandy to London. Nowadays it still serves good pub food and a pleasant selection of lagers and ales.

This map just exuded history. We liked it so much we laid out £300 for it one Sunday afternoon in an "Antiques Fayre" at the exhibition hall at Sandown, the race track between us and Ogleby's Portsmouth Road. A month later we found ourselves early one Friday morning driving down the same road, en route to Normandy. "Why do you want to do that?" our neighbor, Alistair, had asked us before we left.

"It's just across the Channel. We wanted to see what Britain looks like from that side."

"If it were up to me," Alistair said, "I'd give those French wankers two fingers and tell them bugger off."

"Two fingers?" I asked him. I made an indecent gesture at him. "Like this?"

"No, not your standard Yank obscenity. Two fingers. It goes back to the time when the French and English were always at war and the main weapon was the bow and arrows. Maybe 400 years ago? Well, whenever the French took prisoners of our archers, they would chop off the two fingers from their right hands. That way they couldn't shoot an arrow from a bow any more. Legend has it that a group of archers escaped before the French could de-finger them. In the next battle, as they routed the French, they stuck up their two fingers in defiance."

"So how do you feel about the French and all that, 400 years later?"

"Like I said, give them two fingers and tell them to bugger off."

At Portsmouth we drove right on to the P&O Ferry for the four and a half-hour English Channel crossing. Geologists tell us that Britain and France used to be one land mass before continental drift created the Channel. Maybe some residual magnetic forces made Normandy seem to us like only an extension of Surrey.

Or maybe it was just because we could drive there in five hours.

By afternoon we parked in the courtyard of a small hotel in the French town of Bayeaux. "Ah, you are Américain, not British," the proprietor said. "Too bad. You would be able to see in this town the two epic battles for the soul of Britain. This was the first French town to be liberated from the Nazis after D-day. The other battle was fought a little longer ago, about 900 years, and it was across the Channel. But our tapestry tells the story so much better here where it started."

Every guidebook Eileen had read about Normandy called the Bayeaux Tapestry a "must see." We had seen hanging rugs in British castles and French chateau's, in the walled cities in Germany, and even at the plaza in Santa Fe. We may not have been tapestried-out but even then, the Bayeaux Tapestry did not promise to be the highlight of our Normandy weekend. Still we thought we'd give it 20 minutes. After that I wanted to head for the Normandy coast and see some history.

In Britain, tourist concessionaires hand their patrons a piece of paper with a description and send them through their attractions to read for themselves. In Germany, tourists have to wander through on their own. But the French have a way of turning history into an art form. Maybe the same genes that created the great chefs make their way into *les curators* of French museums and historic sites. Bayeaux's curator-chef had done his homework. He kept us in the Bayeaux Tapestry building for two and a half hours.

I had never thought much about 1066 and William the Conqueror and all that. (Another of those "the" people – Eric the Red, Smokey the Bear, Pope John Paul III.) The French version of the story would have me think that William introduced civilized behavior to the British Isles after pushing the savages back to Scotland (where they allegedly remain even today.) The Bayeaux Tapestry records William's conquest. Since it resides in an old seminary, renamed Centre Guillaune-le-Conquèrant, we expected to see it hanging in a great hall. Instead we approached the entrance to a dark passageway where attendants provided us with audio sets, gesturing with soft French murmurs for us to move along. As we entered, the audio sets activated as the episode began in 1064.

Not your traditional hanging rug of faded blues and reds, the Bayeaux Tapestry is a single strip of cloth only a yard tall but 230 feet long. (John Ogleby would have loved it.) Bishop Oddo commissioned it in about 1088 to commemorate W the C's victory over the Brits. If John Ogleby created the first trip-tick, Bishop Oddo was responsible for the first full-length cartoon strip. In 58 scenes, his craftspersons (I don't know if they were men or women.) embroidered detail of the events leading up to the Normans' Channel crossing and their engagement with Britain's army – the advance, retreat, recovery, and eventually the defeat of King Harold.

Cartooning 900 years ago hadn't quite reached digital quality. The characters in the main tableau along the middle looked like a blend of cave glyphs and Doonesbury. Rich detail covered the tapestry's top and bottom edges with mythological characters, Latin script, and foliage. The color scheme, mostly in the sandstone family, could fit nicely in a New Mexico pueblo of the same vintage.

As we wandered along the 230-foot tunnel, we listened at our own pace to each of the 30 or 40 narratives on our audio sets. When we looped back to revisit some previous episode, we could again hear the right narrative for that spot from some cleverly focused radio transmitter. Some people walked briskly through. Some leaned on the protective rail and stared at one section alone. We lingered for over an hour before we moved on to the interpretive center for the "rest of the story."

W the C didn't just say, one Friday afternoon, "Hey, what the heck. Let's invade Britain." The good Bishop Oddo, himself, stood behind the throne and whispered in his ear. The Bishop even rode with him into battle.

Speaking of battle, I had always remembered that 1066 went with the expression "the Battle of Hastings." Eileen has since been to the alleged site of the hostility in East Sussex. W the C landed at the port town of Hastings, but he and his troops didn't find Harold there. Having heard of W the C's amphibious landing on the South Coast, Harold was hustling back from some military escapade in Scotland. That gave William the opportunity to advance about eight kilometers inland from Hastings to engage Harold in a town subsequently called Battle. I supposed historians couldn't bring themselves to call 1066 the Battle of Battle.

His Excellency, the good Bishop, appears prominently in the tapestry at strategic moments, always in a befitting posture. Even amidst the fighting, he carries no weapon and strikes a supplicative pose with eyes heavenward. The historical accounts identify him as the rascal that caused the whole affair as W the C's mentor. The story goes that when Edward the Confessor (the "t" word in the middle again) died, Harold, a despot too unpopular to be called "the anything," jumped in to seize the crown. As Harold tried to get his act together, Oddo the Bishop saw the opportunity to expand his ecclesiastical reach. He convinced his protégé, William, who hadn't conquered anything yet and still had only one name, to invade.

Ironically it all came to no good for O the B. Some years after the victory he presented the tapestry to W the C to ingratiate himself further, but shortly after he rankled him somehow and was tried for treason and executed. Luckily someone had the presence of mind later to stuff the tapestry away in a cathedral in England where it was found about 800 years later.

We tried to ask the museum docents how the tapestry ended up back in a French museum. "Je ne se pais," shrugged the docent.

Later that evening we ate at a small Bayeaux bistro. With the help of another patron who spoke minimal English, we found that the *specialitie de jour* was veal brain and tongue in squid sauce. Despite the gesticulating encouragement from the proprietor, and to his great disappointment, we opted for a bucket of mussels and a bottle of local claret. "Claret?" he exclaimed. "Avec les moules?"

It took several minutes to convince him we really did want red wine with mussels. The attending *garçon* wouldn't even pour for us. "Le Américain ... mumble,

mumble ..." we heard as he saw us commit this venial sin.

"Why do you suppose 1066 and all that commands such fascination in England?" Eileen asked over the dregs of the claret.

"Maybe it's because everywhere we've been, they keep tracing their past back to him. The guidebook says that every British monarch since then has been a descendent of William the Conqueror. Even the House of Windsor, and they used to be the House of Hanover from Germany. I can't figure out how they got Norman blood over to Saxony before they moved to England to take the monarchy. Must have been all that inter-royal hanky-panky and matchmaking."

"Maybe it's the Domesday Book," Eileen offered on a more serious note. "How many Norman churches and buildings have we seen that claim to be in the Domesday Book?"

The Domesday Book, W the C's census in 1086, surveyed all the land holdings and recorded all valuables belonging to every manor in England. Since England was blanketed with the manor system by 1086, that meant virtually every bit of wealth was documented. Anybody living in or otherwise showing off a Domesday Book-recorded structure today, and there are still a lot, lets you know about it right away.

At the end of a bottle of dessert wine with biscuits and a French cheese that could wilt your socks, we concluded with some solemnity that whatever it was that puzzled us would have to be solved some other day.

Sunday, a heavy fog lifted from Bayeaux by mid-morning. We drove north and found Arromanches-les-

Bans, a place where tourists like us can start to engage in the enormity of June 6, 1944. Hours after Operation Overlord began, the Allied assault established a beachhead there on Gold Beach, just east of Omaha and Utah Beaches. The Nazis had expected an invasion would converge on a port city like Le Havre, almost 100 kilometers to the east. They correctly anticipated that success inland would require logistics support. But the Allies had created their own port facilities at the English Coast and towed them to the small harbor at Arromanches to be moored.

The Historic Center at Arromanches documents the slaughterous events that led in June 1944 to a secure gateway to France and commemorates the troops that died there. The center faces the beach and from there we could see half dozen derelict caissons a few hundred yards offshore. They gave us the measure of the real scale of the effort, better than the miniature model in the Center. A film with mostly familiar historic footage gave a frightening reprise of the approach of the troops on the landing craft.

"Do you notice that no one in here is very energized like tourists usually are?" I asked Eileen.

"And the fastest selling souvenirs seem to be the little American and British flags in everyone's hands," she answered. "No 'I love Arromanches' T-shirts. No midget LST key chains. And everyone is so somber. This could be a long day."

We drove west along the empty coast roads. We saw the road signs that lead to the five Allied landing sites that retain their code names to this day – Gold, Juno, Sword, Utah, and Omaha.

"You can almost see the ghosts of the retreating German soldiers and advancing Allies scurrying over these fields," Eileen said as we drove down the empty plains that rolled back from the cliffs above the beaches.

Just past Omaha, signs in English directed us to that notorious site, Ponte du Loc, where the American Rangers assaulted the cliff-top emplacement of big bore guns. We climbed into the damp, ominous bunkers. Through the empty gun ports we could see miles of exposed sandy beach. We walked around the surrounding moonscape, still pockmarked from the unsuccessful naval bombardment and dive-bombing. The entire gun emplacement covered only an area 90 by 120 feet, a target apparently beyond the accuracy of naval guns two kilometers away. Through rusting barbed wire, we peered over the cliff edge, just as the Nazi soldiers must have during the operation. From the top, the position seemed wholly unassailable by frontal assault. How the American Rangers made it up the cliff while the Germans stared down their throats staggered my mind.

A few minutes later in the nearby town of Luc-sur-Mer, we visited a small, privately run exhibition that commemorated the Pont du Loc action. Part way through their movie of more black and white film clips, we started to see interspersed cameos by John Wayne, Robert Wagner, Paul Anka, and Red Buttons. We realized the museum owners had unabashedly mixed original news photography with pirated footage from *The Longest Day*. Still, their creative composition allowed us only a momentary smile.

We stopped for lunch and an emotion break in the seaside town of Courselles-sur-Mer, about a quarter-hour after every other tourist did as well. The proprietors of five overcrowded seafront restaurants turned us away. I developed a panicky feeling that we might find the same thing everywhere in Whatever-sur-Mer and that we might actually miss a meal in this country. In desperation, I drove through the seamier part of town and spotted a tiny waterfront bar. "Let's try one more time," I gasped.

As we walked in, the proprietor gave us a toothless grin from behind the bar. "Do you serve lunch?" I asked slowly.

His grin sagged into a quizzical look. He glanced towards the customers at the bar for help. The three of them turned their palms up and shrugged their shoulders in concert. "Je ne comprends pas."

The proprietor shouted a summons to the back and a fireplug of a woman shuffled to his side and traded the soft cooing sounds of a French conversation with him. Even without our understanding a word, the intimacy made it clear they were husband and wife – and that she was in charge.

I thought I'd take another tack. "Menu?" I repeated several times while I made stupid-looking gestures of scooping something off the bar into my mouth.

The eyes of the denture-challenged proprietor lit up momentarily, but then slid into brownout as he turned up his palms again with a shrug and more dulcet French sounds. He pointed to his watch and clucked a few French hen sounds. Apparently they were getting ready to close. A lightening-swift elbow jab from the fireplug cut short his explanation as his expression turned to terror. "Ah, oui. Le menu," he said, as he miraculously produced a folder from under the bar.

Our newly enervated host assumed the stature of *maître d' hôtel*. He seated us at the window table, all the while glancing nervously at his wife.

I've read that the French favor *pastis* as afternoon refreshment, but I had little idea what *pastis* was. To our grinning host I said, "Pastis, şil vous plait. And saucisse, şil vous plait," pointing to an item on the menu and hoping desperately that I was ordering a drink and sausage.

Eileen, less adventurously ordered *un biér* and *pommes frites* using the same digital selection technique. We both wondered how we would get across the concept of catsup.

Pastis, I found out, comes from that great family of anise-based spirits that remind everyone of chewing penny licorice sticks. *Ouzo* in Greece, *rag*i in Turkey, *sambucco* in Italy – they all taste the same. Not surprisingly, the French take credit for perfecting the drink – Monsieur Paul Ricard had argued for decades that he invented the original in 1932 while the Pernod brothers claimed to have preceded him by four years. A few years earlier, Ricard and Pernod, the two great names in *pastis*, merged into one company and the debate became less acrid.

Pastis has a colorless, oily look. I gathered people dilute it with water because our host, now in the role of *garçon*, brought the liquor in a fluted glass on a tray with a pitcher of water ten times the volume. When I poured in a dash of water, the two liquids emulsified to a gray color closely resembling dishwater.

I could see how *pastis* could be habit forming. It goes down like rainwater into a storm sewer and has an aftertaste like honey, despite the anise base. I could get in a lot of trouble with *pastis*.

Another *pastis* and beer arrived unannounced and *le garçon* jabbed his thumb over his shoulder toward a newly–arrived patron who grinned at us from the bar. Taken aback, I thought I should be gracious.

I lifted the glass toward him and said in my best French, "Merci."

He must have taken this as an invitation because he walked over and sat down. "You are not British, are you?" he said in a thick French accent that made British sound like it had two *e*'s in it.

"No, we're American."

"I am glad. We do not welcome so much zhose beer-drinking hooligans. Zhey are always looking for a bar to fight in. Zee lager louts think zhey still are our heroes from zee war. Well we showed zhem in zee World Cup, no?

"Yes you did, didn't you," I said, glancing furtively at Eileen.

"Well, here comes our food," Eileen exclaimed. "Thank you for the drinks," she said, successfully dispatching him back to the bar.

"Fooking hooligans anglais," he mumbled as he wandered out the door a few minutes later.

My *saucisse* arrived with flare, an eight-inch pork sausage of high quality, served with my own *pommes frites* and mustard. Catsup arrived after but a single request. We had the cafe to ourselves, so we lingered over the simple meal. Out the window and beyond the white sand of Normandy beach, the English Channel glistened in the afternoon sun. Our proprietor-hosts stood together behind the bar. He incessantly wiped imaginary droplets from the bar top. She stood with head cocked and her hands clasped at her ample bosom, waiting patiently. Together they made a portrait of the French cousins of the American Gothic.

In a mellow mood we left, but not before a profusion of "*merci*'s" and hand shaking, as if we had just betrothed our virgin daughter to their idiot son. "Who says the French are unpleasant to American tourists?" Eileen asked me.

A 20-minute ride up the coast delivered us to Ranville, one of a tragic series of American cemeteries across Western Europe. We strolled down the neatly graveled walk that took us past a treed bluff overlooking the Channel, then to endless acres of white crosses. We noticed visitors wandering over the gravesites and wondered if that wasn't a desecration, but in a few minutes we joined them as well. Like an infinity of tourists before me, I squatted with my camera and caught the geometry of receding parallel and intersecting lines of crosses.

"You know," I said to Eileen, "with all these people wandering around here taking pictures, just like us, this could turn into a tourist destination instead of a memorial. Before we let this glum thought depress us, we turned back towards the entrance to make our way through the matrix of crosses. Eileen stopped for a moment and pointed to a nameplate. "Look. John Doherty, Houston, Texas. Born April 1, 1924, died June 18, 1944. And this one, Silvio Antonini, New York, died, June 10, 1944."

We took turns reading names and dates and hometowns, many places where we had lived or visited. Gradually the reality dawned on us that we stood on the graves of real people – Americans with real names from actual places. Birth dates between 1916 and 1926 prevailed, deaths from the sixth of June 1944 through just a few ensuing weeks. A few days in June and July showed up much more frequently than any others.

Any theme park notion we had gave way to a sobering, almost embarrassing realization of sacrifice and futility. The lives of so many sons and fathers had abruptly ended on the battlefields here. The carnage was so intense and enduring that America couldn't even divert the resources to return the remains of the dead to the mothers and wives back home. So here they lay, as their own memorial.

We left the American Cemetery in a gloomy mood. Our guidebook recommended one more stop. About 12 kilometers away in St. Laurent-sur-Mer, the Germans had their own cemetery. It seemed strange that the French would tolerate on their soil a memorial to fallen Nazi soldiers.

If the American cemetery at Ranville left an impression of sober dignity, the German's graveyard gave us the creeps. We entered through a narrow, crypt-like building and immediately faced a macabre, black marble monument in the center of a field of black crosses and grave markers. Malevolence and dread floated in the air. Only someone with a Darth Vader complex could want to linger in a grim setting like this.

"Take a picture and let's get out of here," Eileen said. "I don't know what the Germans had in mind when they designed this place, but I think the French have their final revenge here. They must be trying to make any Germans visiting here to pay respects come away with a feeling of reproach and maybe remorse."

We finished our two-day tour of those historic conflicts in the dining room of the ferry that night, on our way back to Surrey. "We'll both have the, er, fish," I said with my finger again on the menu. Trying to pronounce *Le filet de turbot poele auberre de Montpelier et huitre de Bouzigues grilles* would only embarrass me. And in another gesture of oenophilic arrogance, I violated the sensitivities of yet another sommelier. "And we'll have a bottle of the ninety-two Bordeaux."

We ruminated over the weekend's experience and concluded that the two make-or-break battles that had just engaged us so thoroughly bracket most of the important history of Britain.

"1066 and 1944 are like bookends," I noted in an unexpected moment of erudition, after our noses had been in the Bordeaux for a while. "Not much of note happened before 1066 and not much good has happened to Britain since WW II."

"They voted Margaret Thatcher out of office."

"Well, there's that."

During a Sunday pub walk a week later, Alistair pointed out to us that 1066 was the last time a foreign power successfully invaded British soil.

"Wimbledon starts in a few days," I told him. "Perhaps a small wager about Britain's extraordinary impregnability…?"

*****

I read in the *Times* a week later that Monsieur Ricard, age 88, died in his sleep the night before, ending yet another battle.

June 15

Dear Richard,

In case you think I'm on a perpetual high here in jolly olde England, THIS PLACE SUCKS! I'd like to shove the place right down their jolly olde throats. I can't stand to listen to their stupid excuses and their nit-picky rules.

Well from that you might have guessed I failed my driving test. The examiner nixed me because I was going *too slow*. He told Mr. Goodpasture afterwards that I should have passed a bicyclist riding in front of me. When I heard that I ran back over and yelled, "Pass him? There was a double line in the middle. Cars parked on both sides and oncoming traffic. Are you crazy? Somehow the compelling logic of my appeal failed to move him to reverse his decision. "I'm certain, missus, that everyone would move over. You can't detain traffic like that," he said. Now I have to sign up for another test (for another £25) and take another lesson (£16). And worst of all I have to put a decal on the back of our car with a big red L on it to indicate I'm a learner (or is it loser?) who has flunked the driver's test. And the decal cost four pounds fifty.

Over the weekend we went to Ovington-near-Alresford where our American friends, Ginnie and Jack live. This little hamlet deep in the forest has only 28 homes, a church, and a pub. It was jammed when we went there Sunday (the pub, not the church.) The most dangerous time to drive in rural Britain must be Sunday afternoons between 2:00 and 3:00. Everyone has been to Sunday Roast at the pub, washing it down with copious volumes of lager or ale. Then they drive home for a nap.

Ginnie and Jack live in a 500-year old house formerly inhabited by medieval midgets. The ceilings are so low Bill's head brushed the heavy beams in the reception rooms. When I got up in the middle of the night to go to the bathroom I forgot to duck when I went down the short staircase and hit my head so hard I fell backwards on the floor, stunned for a few minutes. Jack was unmoved the next morning. "Didn't you see the little brass sign on the beam that says 'Mind your head'?" I told him that's what I hit my head on. I've still got a bruise and headache.

While we were down there we did learn to appreciate the power shower our landlords had installed for us in Michael Court. Ginnie's house has an "ordinary" shower that works about as well as standing under a coffee can of hot water with holes punched in the bottom. Hard to get wet in all the right places.

This morning I went to Claygate at 8:15 to assure I'd be able to get some scones. There were no baked goods at all on the shelves. I asked the counter lady what happened. "Oh, Monday is baker's day off." Grrrr.

Love, your frustrated sister

5

Pomp, Circumstance, and Mac

"I'll go if you promise to get tickets to Wimbledon."

Eileen had given me this perilous ultimatum before we committed to come to England. Of course I giddily agreed. By late April, two months before Wimbledon, I had begun to panic about that irresponsible covenant and started to call the scalpers.

"A hundred and thirty quid for an opening weekday, mate. Per ticket."

"What happens if it rains on the day I have my tickets?" I asked. "Do I get a raincheck?"

"Afraid not, mate. You just get washed out. That's Wimbledon."

Daunted by the threat of four hundred U.S. dollars worth of soggy tickets and no tennis, I suggested to Eileen she consider offering the ticket takers certain personal services for access to the matches. At this moment of marital crisis, our telephone rang.

"Laffler. Dorsey. Put your wife on the phone." It was an old college buddy. He worked for one of those big international oil companies and I could tell from our side of the conversation that we were going to share one of his perks.

"Wimbledon… of course… whenever… Doesn't matter – Bill will take off from work," Eileen said into the phone, with a wide-eyed expression of hope.

Dorsey had been one of Eileen's targets as soon as we had arrived in Britain and her incessant hints finally paid off. Dorsey had four corporate tickets for the sixth day of the fortnight, the first Saturday of play.

The national sport of Britain may be football (a.k.a. soccer), but Wimbledon is a public celebration. Even the royalty show up, a dozen or more at a time. They sit in their venerably placed box at Center Court. They are but fifty feet from rows of the bourgeois fans, most of whom act as courtiers should, and as the rules of conduct suggest on the Wimbledon ticket envelopes – *It is polite to acknowledge a well-executed shot with applause, but please, no clapping at double faults.* Occasionally a few riff-raff make it through the security, however, and boos and catcalls have assaulted the royal ears more than once in recent years.

Of course, disaster is more likely than not to strike this festival and its ticket holders. I don't mean the IRA bomb threats that had long-since convinced the police to shut down the car parks near the tennis complex. That was minor compared to the possibility of a rainout. Even the big corporate spenders don't get rainchecks. So imagine the thorough distress in our household when the fortnight finally arrived and sporadic rain fell on day one and only two full rounds of tennis were completed. Day two, drenching torrents ended a five-month drought in Southern England. With the possible exception of the head of the Thames Water District, all England watched the skies with dismay.

Wednesday was washed out except for an hour of late afternoon matches.

Thursday, wet. Not one match started.

Friday, same as Thursday.

The front page of Friday's Evening Standard lamented that not this many matches had been rain-delayed since 1981. We went to see Bill Cosby, on-stage at Leicester Square in London on Friday night. "You people in England need to calm down over this tennis thing," he scoffed. "Think what the rain does for the little people, like the 428th seed. 'Dear Mom, here it is Monday of the second week of the fortnight, and I still haven't been eliminated from Wimbledon...'"

In unparalleled despair, we set out on Saturday morning for the 10:30 opening gate. As we left the house, it began to rain.

About three-quarters of a mile from the main gate was a sight not seen by Americans since the breadlines of the Great Depression. Wet, cold wretches shuffled languidly along the sidewalk in a line. Hundreds of them, maybe thousands. It was "The Queue," the unquestionably deranged fanatics who had spent the afternoon, evening, and night before in the cold, darkness, and rain to buy that day's tickets to Wimbledon. But unlike the depressed and unemployed of the thirties, they each had a semblance of smile, some slack-jawed, but others beaming with anticipation, as they sloshed toward their Elysian fields. Insanity.

Our corporate passes entitled us to a reserved parking space, and a friendly official pointed us past a large Wimbledon Golf Club sign into a sodden slough laid with plywood decking. "Follow the signposts to 'Wade.' It's on the fifth fairway," he told us.

Wade, I wondered, as we drove into the swampy meadow. Probably better than being assigned to Swim.

Should we have worn our wellies? Will we have to roll up our pants legs and make for high ground?

Everything, it turns out, even their car parks, gets named for Wimbledonians of past glory, even Virginia Wade. Before the day was over, I hoped to find the Jimmy Connors toilets and the John McEnroe complaint window.

By 10:30, as we entered the complex, the rain had slowed to a count-the-drops rate, a good sign, but not enough to make us optimistic. Still, the atmosphere inside was more like a dazzlingly medieval fair than a tennis tournament. Officials with gaily color rainsuits wandered about with large "Information" signs protruding over their heads. Buskers dished out strawberries and cream ("Vanilla yogurt substitute now available") in one kiosk, bangers and eggs in another. Under the ubiquitous *i*, little old ladies with patient smiles staffed the information booth. As we stood in line I heard them say for probably the hundredth time that morning, "Court Three is down to the right, then straight-away,"

"Museum? Directly behind you, dear," she said to us, without the slightest intimation that we were totally unobservant oafs, which of course we were.

"We have to go to the Wimbledon shop and get a memento," Eileen told me. "And maybe a Christmas gift or two."

Innovation at the All England Lawn Tennis & Croquet Club moves slowly. Not till recently did they corrupt their heritage and dignity by commercializing the Wimbledon logo. Thus, an insufficiently quick pass through the Wimbledon shop netted us two sweaters, three tennis towels (two from last year but reduced to just ten pounds each), two shirts, and one hat. Each had the Wimbledon insignia, which accounted for most of the £240 tab.

By noon we had rendezvoused with Dorsey and wife Susan at our seats in Centre Court, awaiting the verdict on the weather. At 12:01 the official announcement came that play would commence in fifteen minutes. The grounds crews rolled back the canvas tarps to the crowd's ovation. The ballpersons and linespersons took their positions, and the notorious Bruno Magli, umpire for this match, solemnly ascended to his chair. Magli, apparently one of the most respected umpires, had officiated the infamous Jeff Terango match in a prior year, the one that prompted Terango's wife to sock Bruno unceremoniously in the choppers because of her rage at the lively on-court altercation between her husband and him. Ahh, let the games begin... please, before it rains again.

There were two highlight matches that afternoon. The first took only twenty-five minutes as Martina Hingis, the young Swiss with a perpetually frozen smile, completed her rain-delayed match with the somewhat older Olga Barabanshikova from Belarus. How do they fit that name on her plane tickets? Hingis finished off the Belaruski in short order, but I noticed that despite Hingis' clearly superior prowess, the crowd was giving inordinate attention to Miss Barabanshikova.

You've watched the audience in a tennis match and seen the spectators sitting along the sidelines. Their heads wag back and forth as the players rally the ball. In this match, a sizable number of the heads stayed with Barabanshikova. After a few games I realized that she was sporting a new style of tennis panties under her tennis dress, cut more like a thong then the traditional tennis wear. Every serve or overhead she hit created a palpable vacuum in Centre Court as ten thousand males drew a short breath. Alas, Hingis won handily, and Barabanshikova was to seen no more, to the chagrin of her fans but to the relief of the tongue-twisted announcers.

Tennis was not at the top of the list of things that Dorsey liked to do. At the end of the teenage Hingis – flashing Barabanshikova match, he herded us to the Debenture Lounge for lunch, even though the next match would begin shortly. The corporate citizens who hold the Debenture tickets purchase the series for about £9000. Per seat. That includes all the matches you can bear to watch over the fortnight, reserved parking places (my spot in "Wade"), and access to the Debenture Lounge. There a Debenture Ticket holder can purchase a meal, and if he's nimble enough, get a table overlooking three or four outside courts where play is usually continuous.

So off we went to the Debenture Lounge, located conveniently about 150 feet from our Debenture Seats. Guards manned the door; thick carpets covered the floor. "Strawberries and cream and champagne – that's what we've got to have," Dorsey proclaimed, as he nabbed one of the regally appointed window tables, overlooking a men's singles match. To my surprise, at the far end of the room patrons queued incongruously in a cafeteria line, trays in hand, heading for the steam tables. Undoubtedly the Lounge was designed for the serious fan – fast turnover and a quick return to the matches.

As a preemptive strike I blurted out, "What kind of champagne will you have?" I felt compelled to reciprocate for this day at the matches and Dorsey graciously let me pay. The bill for our light lunch came to £110 pounds, including £50 for the bottle of champagne. So far Wimbledon had cost us £350 pounds and we'd seen only one match.

By the time we returned to our seats, the match of the day was already at the 3-2 score. Tim Henman faced the Frenchman, Golmard. Henman, by then referred to widely as "Our Tim," was England's brightest star. Our Tim had been struggling for fame and fortune on the international circuit for several years, but going into this Wimbledon he seemed in top form, according to the sports writers. The media had whipped all England into a fever over the prospects of a Brit in the finals.

No one ever used the word charismatic when they described Our Tim. "Proper lad," Alistair had told me over a couple of cooled Boddingtons at the pub the Sunday before. "He looks like the head boy in public school sixth form. He'd dribble tea on his tie before he'd ever wear one of those baseball caps with the bill in the back like the Aussies do."

"Public school sixth form?" I asked him.

"Upper classman in what you call private school in America – Eton, Exeter.'"

All this referred to Our Tim's fetchingly clean-cut demeanor and fresh-faced smile. He also had that sort of perpetually vacant stare that contact lens wearers or toll road cashiers sometimes have.

The fans had turned out for Our Tim. They were decked in Britannia – hats, and shirts, and face paint showing the unmistakable Union Jack stripes. Six endlessly noisy girls in the bleachers had one each of the six letters of his name stenciled on their faces. Even louder were the crowd's responses to the crucial points. A throaty moan rumbled through the stadium when Golmard placed an unreachable dropshot inside the service line, followed by a suffering mother's sigh when Our Tim hit a ball into the net. A deep resonance starting in 30,000 viscera, climaxed in commodious tumult and standing ovation when Tim passed Golmard at the net on his return of serve to win the first set.

Even the Royal Box filled up by the end of the third set, as Tim had moved ahead by two. Absent today were the Duke and Duchess of Kent, whose main public function seems to be once a year at Wimbledon representing 1000 years of royal succession. But the Royal Seats were dutifully filled with other personages of no doubt equal import. The scene was resplendent with class – coifed hair for the ladies; the required raspberry colored suit; coats, waistcoats, and cravats for the gentlemen; grandsons with combed hair and white shirts and ties. The box, which could hold about 25, was sprinkled with the gray-haired and long in tooth; invited foreign aristocracy, evident by their color or costume; and the eminently rich and famous, just obvious from looking at them. All watched in the characteristic style of the nobility, heads down, eyes looking through the uppermost level of their trifocals, even the ones who didn't wear glasses.

In the fourth set, with Tim about to lose two in a row, the oldest of them succumbed to the champagne glow and the warmth of lap blankets. They dropped off for a Royal Snooze. They resembled a late afternoon session in the House of Lords, with two or three of the dozing gents inviting the local finches to nest in their gaping mouths, another teetering on the edge of his chair, in danger of sliding off his cane on to the floor.

By the fifth set, everyone was thoroughly re-engaged with the match. With Our Tim at the service line, the audience had to be continually reminded by Bruno: "Quiet please. The players are ready."

But the crowd could not contain their urge to urge, "C'mawn Tim. Yew kin do wit."

Rising to their demands, Tim fought off three match points in the fifth set, broke the demoralized Golmard with his final passing shot, and took game, set, and match. With his racquet clenched in one hand and the other in a fist and his laddish face flushed with victory, Our Tim gestured heroically at the crowds, at his parents in the family box, and at the absent Duke and Duchess.

Tennis was meant to be played in the daylight, according to British tradition, so Wimbledon has no night lights. When the sun goes down, the players quit. And on a cloudy day at the end of June, dusk comes at 8:40 PM. In the final match of the day, the near defeat of Monica Seles by the obscure American teenager, Karen Brandi, was postponed till the morrow … and evaporated when Brandi withered the next morning before the re-charged Seles.

We gathered up our booty, and left for our car. Dorsey and wife had already departed, muttering something about an aching lumbar, a dinner engagement, and traffic. We were the last car to leave the bog called "Wade" and let our car follow the ruts to the highway. We saw hundreds of people had lined up in the Queue.

Due to the week's deluges, the tournament officials declared the next day to be People's Sunday. Rarely does official play take place on Sunday. No Sunday tickets are ever sold. So, when the weather demands it, the British get a treat – People's Sunday. That day everyone gets their seat in the All England Tennis and Croquet Club Sunday by joining the Queue. Henman played his next match before a rowdy SRO Centre Court that made the crowds at head-bashing rugby matches look like teatime at the Savoy. They whistled, cheered, and catcalled, practices explicitly forbidden by the decorum further articulated on the ticket folders. But of course, it being People's Sunday, no one had ticket folders. The fans went berserk and danced in the aisles when Our Tim won the final rally.

What a glorious day for England, as the crowd glowingly acclaimed their new hero, "Hen-man clap-clap-clap. Hen-man clap-clap-clap."

Thank heavens the Duchess stayed home.

Tuesday, Henman went on to beat the reigning champion, Michael Stich. But in the quarterfinals, an inexplicably lethargic Centre Court crowd filled only two-thirds of the stadium while Henman went tragically down in flames. His two countrymen instinctively followed him into the turf in the same round, and once again, upholding a long tradition, no Brits made it to the semifinals. At the end of the fortnight, Pete Sampras brought the champion's cup back to America.

Unperturbed, Alistair bought a round of Boddington at the pub the following Sunday. "I hope you appreciate how the British Government, in their own subtle way, has recognized the perennial dominance of Americans at Wimbledon in the last few decades," he said.

"How's that?" I asked.

Alistair selected a five and a ten pound note from his wallet and folded them lengthwise, one with an irreverent crease across the Queen's nose, the other over Michael Faraday's. "There," he said, splicing them together. "Your most notorious player from the 1970s."

June 30

Dear Richard,

The outdoors social season is here. I went to the races at Ascot with a bunch of the American ladies. Everybody dresses very formally, the men in gray morning coats, the ladies in flowery dresses and big hats. (When I was back in Texas last month for a short visit I bought my big hat at Nieman's. Since I couldn't pack it I wore it back. While I was waiting on line at the airport I noticed this young cowboy behind me staring at it. He finally said to me, "That's a mighty fine hat you got there, ma'am." I told him I was taking it to Britain because everyone wears hats like these at the Ascot Raceway. "I sure would like to see a sight like that, ma'am," he said.

I heard through the American grapevine that we could get tickets to the Henley crew races. So I called the number someone gave me and asked a pleasant lady if there were tickets for visiting Americans. "Well, perhaps, but you must present your case in writing to the Board." So I made up some elaborate letter about how we enjoyed their traditions and all, and five days later we got four tickets.

That's not the best part. I was carpooling to a tennis team match yesterday with Lulu and a lady from one of the big manor houses in Ripley. She must have been slumming that day. Anyway, the subject of Henley came up – her son from Eton was going to row there – and I told her we had tickets. She went into the standard spiel I'd already heard about the dress code – women's hem at least one inch below the knee, men in blazers, ties, and flannels. I told her it all sounds like fun and we might catch up with them there. "I really don't think so. Where are your tickets?" I told her it was something called the Steward's Enclosure. Horrified, she asked, "Did you get them from a Steward?" I told no, that I just wrote some B.S. note and they sent them to me. "Well, that's certainly unorthodox," she spluttered, totally flummoxed. "My **husband** is a Steward. I'll have to report that to him."

I passed my driver's test and now own a British Drivers License (£15), so I have stripped the red L decal from our back bumper. Ginnie sent me a congratulation card. On the front it had "Bloody L. You've made it, mate."

Whole episode cost me £170. Incredible. What do poor people do?

They Just Don't Get It #2: I saw a sign in London, "Bargain Basement," and the arrow was pointing upstairs.

TJDGI # 3: No matter how hot we get after tennis, the girls always adjourn to the grille for a "proper" pot of tea, which means steaming hot. And they get as agitated as wet hens if the full accompaniment is not provided – the tiny spoons, the extra pot of hot water, and so on. All the while I'm dying for a cold Diet Coke, but I go along.

Love, your amused sister

6

Picnic

"Hey Laffler. Y'all want to go to Glyndebourne?" It was Dorsey again, calling from America this time and in the process of moving back there. In the thirty-five years I've known him, he's never learned to spell or pronounce my name. "We're flying back in on the ninth and we can git us four tickets on the tenth. You wanna go?"

It didn't take me two seconds to accept this unexpected opportunity to see close up the wellborn on their own turf. Curt and Marie-Hèléne, neighbors in the close and our cultural advisors, had told us of the delights of Glyndebourne. The great and beautiful people of England say *Glyndebourne* with hushed reverence. For years they have driven their Bentleys, and Jags down the M-3 from London to the south of Kent on warm summer afternoons to enjoy superb opera performed in a country opera house. As an added attraction, they get to bring their suppers with them and picnic on the front lawn and in intimate crannies of the surrounding gardens.

"Strictly black tie," warned Dorsey. "Fancy stuff for the ladies. You got a tux? How about a picnic table?"

I promised we could handle it all and invited him and Susan to stay with us the night before.

At ten p.m. two weeks later, the doorbell rang. "Stash this stuff in your fridge, Laffler, and then put me to bed," said Dorsey. "We need to start early on picnic preparation." He had piled sacks of green groceries, dairy products, meats and cheeses, and liters of assorted spirits on our stoop. "And oh, here's your tickets."

I looked at the tickets and saw the number 120 next to the words *Le Comte Ory*. I thought to myself that probably means seat 12 in row O or seat 20 in row I. "How much do I owe you?"

"Whatever it says. I think they're about £120 pounds each," he said. Ouch. While I wrote out the check for £240, I decided not to spoil the show for Eileen by telling her we were about to go to a $400 show.

At 7:30 the next morning, we awoke to the sounds of clunking pots and kitchenware. Dorsey was already at it. I padded down to see the damage. Bowls of things were marinating on the breakfast table and steam rose from pots on the cooker.

"Good morning. Where's your red vermouth?" he asked.

"Manhattans this early in the morning?"

"Maybe later. I need two ounces for these cheese balls."

Dorsey continued uninterrupted with his mixing and chopping. He stripped the papery shells from cloves of garlic to roast them. He sliced shallots razor-thin to add to the potato salad. Next to a tray of kippers in the fridge he cooled freshly boiled eggs and capers while he chopped his fresh dill to sprinkle on the smoked Scottish salmon. The whole place smelled like a Jewish delicatessen on the Lower East Side.

"Are we going to bring any regular food in case we get hungry," I asked him.

"This is regular food where we're going. Ain't no cheeseburgers at Glyndebourne."

In mid-afternoon we stowed packages and containers in our cooler and tableware in our wicker basket, loaded up the estate wagon, and left for the south of Kent. The staff at Glyndebourne is astute enough to know that patrons in formalwear don't want to be seen slogging through the car parks lugging coolers and lawn chairs. So they provide an ample supply of local lads dressed in green waistcoats and tight black trousers. At the designated drop zone they will unload the various *impedimenta.* Then they follow the ladies as they wander among the greenery, searching out the perfect site, while the men attend to the more mundane search for the perfect parking place. Both sexes prefer this division of labor.

We set up our table and covered it with white linens, our best silverware, and china. Eileen had put her foot down at the crystalware. "Have you lost it? Haul our Waterford around in a wicker basket. We'll stick to the Walmartware and then we won't worry about breaking a few. Stuff won't taste any different anyway."

Around us a living Monet materialized ... or was it Manet? Tuxedoed gentlemen lit candelabra, poured champagne, and held chairs for their ladies. Women laid out dishes of *foie gras*, gooey Brie, and hard Cheshire. A few meters from us a frail little man unfolded an extravagantly complicated mass of aluminum tubing and sheet metal. He tugged and shoved and banged it on the ground. A table for two emerged, complete with benches. His female companion settled her enormous bottom on one bench as we held our breath. If the table legs hadn't been firmly planted, the poor man would have been catapulted across the Channel to Dunkirk. The braces and fasteners held and the two of them raised their champagne flutes to each other and began their starters.

"Let's have our salmon and Brut and then take a walk," Dorsey suggested as he eased the cork out.

In formal affairs like this, men have it easy. A tux is a tux, even if it is a little tatty at the edges. A few men dared to have a turquoise or yellow plaid bow tie and cummerbund in celebration of summer. One gent wore a scarlet tartan kilt with evening jacket, making his own statement. But the rest of the male population were clones – proper in their sameness, uniform in their display of finery.

On the other hand, the women, for the most part, haplessly failed to make it to chic. Their standard formula included a blue blazer atop a wayworn dress of blue-flowered material of the kind most often seen covering a couch, and of course, sensible shoes. Oh there was an occasional slinky long gown here and there – they invariably were conversing in French – but why are the Brits so preposterously feckless when it comes to fashion? Of course maybe they have to resort to upholstery material to cover those big butts. (There, I've said it, and shame on me for being so snide. It's the Brits that are supposed to be snobs, not Americans.)

If *Le Comte Ory* were sung in English and not Italian, it could have played in London's West End as a British farce. The plot is as thin as the Cheshire cheese slices we had just seen, but the whole show is about body language. The lascivious Count drooled with exceptional amour at the virginal but gullible Lady Adèle throughout the first act.

At the drop of the intermission curtain, we joined the other five hundred frenetically exiting the hall. We had but 70 minutes to eat our main course before the doors to the second act closed. We rushed like lemmings down the grand staircase to the front lawn, passing tables laden with bowls of seafood and pasta, platters of smoked tongue, Yorkshire ham, and Angus beef, and cold roasted vegetables. Corks popped from bottles of Gamay Beaujolais and chilled Gavi di Gavi. We settled into our lobster and scallop medley accompanied by sliced mozzarella, tomato, and avocado.

In another half-hour, deep dishes of trifle and trays of brandy-soaked sponge cake appeared, however fleetingly. Mocha-flavored coffee, still hot from flasks, washed down the sweets to make room for cheese and biscuits and half bottles of after-dinner wine.

With just 15 minutes to go, men and women groaned to their feet and began tossing the leavings wantonly into coolers and wickers. Like penguins fleeing a melting iceberg, the tuxedos rushed through the hedges hauling the remnants of this orgy towards the car parks. The women made their way to the ever-inadequate Ladies WC. With unembarrassed urgency, 500 people relieved themselves and returned to their seats in time to hear the end of the orchestra's foreplay to the second act.

Rossini may not have had Glyndebourne in mind when he wrote that second act, but certainly the resident director did. Consider the fact that the audience has just consumed nearly a thousand pounds of assorted fats, sugars, and carbohydrates, drunk nearly six hundred liters of spirits, and it was nine o'clock at night. The first thing he does is stage a nude scene with the servant girls bathing Lady Adèle's ladies-in-waiting while they sing a song of ungratified desire. That captures at least half the audience. The rest get taken in towards the end as the Count and eight of his henchmen, thinly disguised as mustachioed nuns, played grab-ass with each other and then with Lady Adèle's sweet smelling court. After a clamorous finale involving much hugging and pledges of eternal fidelity, the audience wallowed to their feet to demand two curtain calls.

The night at Glyndebourne was an icon to the privileges of class. The last evidence of that came after we rolled in convoy out of the car park onto the M-3.

"Hey Laffler. You notice there's not one cop in the area?"

Dorsey was right. I hadn't seen one patrol car. This was in a country where the police routinely set up roadblocks during the Christmas season to give breathalyzer tests and where they wait in their cars outside railroad stations to prey on late night diners returning from London. But at Glyndebourne, not a bobby was to be found.

"Hemingway was right, you know," I said to Dorsey. "The rich are different than you and me."

"How's that?"

"They have more money."

July 25

Dear Richard,

Constable Woosely just left again. He came to investigate the windows in our garage that someone broke last week. We now have an addendum to our Case Number 625. The Constable was most upset that this should be happening to the country's guests. And yes, he does take tea.

My tennis partner, Lulu, is about the same age as our middle son. When she found out, she blurted, "I'm just gobsmacked." Now she's taken to calling me Granny. She finally got us a game with some of the "big girls" on the A team. We played them yesterday. One of them is know as The Doe because of the way she struts around the club, gold jewelry around her neck and wrists and fingers. Anyway we had them 5-0 in the first set and the Doe stopped the play. "My tennis elbow is hurting ever so much. Could we take a rain check?" A little later Lulu said to me, "Tennis elbow, my ass. The bitch just couldn't stand being buggered by a D team." Lulu has an irreverent view of social status, despite being brought up in the estate section of Ripley.

The Brits do like to picnic. First we did the one at Glyndbourne, then at Henley. This year's picnic in our Close was on the Fourth of July so Bill talked all the neighbors into a big celebration called Close Encounters of the Fourth Kind. He organized games in the back yards, er, gardens – boules, croquette, ping pong – and was going to have a tennis tournament on the court at Cobwebs (the house across the close) but moss was growing on the surface due to all the rain. Since it was the Fourth, Alistair decorated the croquette pitch in his garden with American and British flags. Everyone kept coming up to us saying congratulations on our independence. The evening ended with a big picnic in the middle of the street. One lady said that she hoped she wouldn't get as pissed as she did last year. I asked her what had made her mad. She paused a minute and then took my hand and said, "Oh no, my dear. Pissed. Drunk. Snockered. Not mad."

Well, she did anyway, as did everyone else. DWI offenses are treated harshly here, so more often than not, partygoers hire a chauffeured car to take them home. "'S a bloody good thing they don't take our license away for walking inder the unfluence," Alistair mumbled late that night, as he tottered homeward across the close. "Otherwise we'd all have to hire wheelchairs with drivers."

TJDGI #4: I love how the Brits are obsessed with freshness. Fresh flowers, fresh fruit, fresh everything. But now I've found the ultimate. I bought a dozen eggs the other day and was puzzled that the carton had no date on it. When I opened it, I saw that each egg had stamped on it, "Best before August 2."

Love, your merrymaking sister

Romancing the Scone

7

Tattoo

I always thought a military tattoo was a globe and anchor emblazoned with "Semper Fi" on the arm of a retired Marine. The Scots have a different idea, and I like it better.

Strictly speaking, Britain consists of four entities, England, Wales, Scotland, and Northern Ireland, so when I refer to Brits, I should be including the Scots, the Welsh, and the Northern Irish along with the English. Well, it doesn't take a minute's conversation with a Scot to learn this preposterous notion was but a political ploy originating in the vicinity of Westminster Abbey. Still, the Scots and the English have been living on the same island in an intimate relationship for a millennium. We decided we needed to find out how different a Scottish Brit was from an English Brit. So, at the end of July we took a weekend break to Edinburgh, Scotland (pronounced *ed'n-bro*, we found out. Not *ed-in- berg* or *ed-in-boro*. And with a burr on the *r*.)

People who travel anywhere in the British Isles the first weekend in August deserve what they get. The cities, the countryside, the towns, the roads, and the hotels are crawling with millions of American, German, and Dutch tourists. But Britain has a fine institution, the local tourist bureau. For about two pounds, they will find you a nearby bed & breakfast, regardless of the notice you give them or the price range you specify. In the past, we'd always had luck, so we resorted to them again.

The closest bed they could find near Edinburgh lay 11 miles from the city center – the Original Hotel in Roslin. With a name like that, we thought there were two possibilities. It had to have some redeeming qualities to keep attracting a clientele. On the other hand, Eileen pointed out ominously, it had a vacancy on the biggest weekend of the year.

With some reservations about our reservation, we made our way, via British Air and Hertz to Roslin. Two features distinguish this modest town. First, every structure is made of stone block, including the two hotels (which count as the second feature). Architects must run out of clever ways to design stone block buildings after about the third one. The two hotels, which inexplicably face each other on the only street in Roslin, are different from each other but almost every other building looks like one of the two. Graying sandstone or granite block construction prevails in Northern Scotland. The buildings secrete an eerie cold feeling, especially in the long nights of winter. On a trip to Aberdeen one evening the previous January, I stood in the center of town with the wind bouncing off the lifeless gray façades, chilling my bones. I felt as if I were in Gotham City. I kept glancing at the low-hanging clouds, expecting to see the Bat-logo beckoning the Dynamic Duo to action.

This particular night in Roslin gave me the same feeling, not the least because on this first day of August, the temperature at 9 pm was only 14° C. Luckily both Eileen and I were smart enough to bring our sweaters. Wool in August. Back home we didn't even wear wool sweaters at Christmas.

My empirical research leads me to believe that every country hotel built in Britain was finished before 1825. I've not come across a younger one. The owners of the Original Hotel missed a public relations opportunity. They should have called this the Newest Hotel because the keystone above the entrance announced that it was built in 1824. The Glen Rosslyn across the street boasted 1818. Apparently after 1818, some phonetically fanatic cartographer decided to simplify the town's name to Roslin, probably to the chagrin of the descendants of the Earl of Rosslyn. A grave marker in the nearby cemetery indicated he died about 1120 after a long, rewarding life of flogging serfs and expropriating lands. His direct, but less prosperous descendent, the present Earl of Rosslyn, was the current Chief Constable of the district. If this town has a long memory, he might do well not to find himself too far from home after dark

Small country hotels in Britain have a simple formula. The front desk is a pile of papers on a stand at the end of a dim hallway. Usually a small sign next to a chrome bell orders me to ring for service, because no one is to be seen. At the summoning, the attending receptionist invariably responds with utter confusion and a sense of disbelief that we have booked a room for the evening. After effusive paper shuffling, the incredulity disappears with "Ah yes, Mr. and Mrs. Lessler, I believe?"

Eileen and I both suffer from a congenital "fiff." We are perpetually unable to communicate over the phone that our last name has two f's in it, not two s's.

We have tried novel approaches. "L-E-F-F, like in Frank, L-E-R." We arrive to find a room booked for Frank Lessler. If I didn't have to use a credit card or leave tracks where I'm staying in case someone needs me, I'd book every time under the name Joe Bleaux.

The second part of the formula is found in the restaurant. Hotels in country towns are hopelessly committed to provide sustenance to their guests. In most cases, the two-hotel village of Roslin being no exception, no other eating establishments can be found for miles. The circumstances demand unachievable performance of the hotel manager. After all, how can he hope to retain the services of a chef with any imagination whatsoever if he only prepares six to ten dinners a week night, and maybe 20 on the weekends? The answer is he doesn't, and "British Cuisine" is the same kind of oxymoron as the "Certified Public Account's Gala Ball" we saw advertised on the hotel announcement board.

What these restaurants lack in culinary achievement they compensate for in flair. Before seating us in dining room, they asked – or really required – us to relax in a small anteroom over an *apéritif.* The drink came with a menu and dish of hot *hors d'ouvres* – warm goat cheese, deep fried meat cakes, and the like. Shortly, they took our dinner order. In about 10 minutes, they moved us to an intimate dining room of white linened tables strewn with silverware and wineglasses. The waitstaff then did the enchantingly elegant Cutlery Shuffle. Holding a tray with a large selection of tableware, they wended their way around us, changing out knives if we ordered fish, spoons if we ordered soup, forks if we ordered salad, stemware for the wine. Immediately after they brought the first course, which surprised us since we were not used to being served the moment we sat at the table. But of course we forgot we did our waiting in the anteroom. Perhaps this entertaining protocol is meant to distract us from the limited selection of "Savory Favourites," the fried lamb cutlets with cauliflower and boiled new potatoes or the broiled plaice with cream sauce and Brussels sprouts.

The remarkable constancy of the sleeping rooms completes the standard country hotel formula: dark, to the point of dingy, small to the point of humorous. Someone in the UK must publish a standard guide to appointing country hotel rooms. The bedspreads and carpeting had indistinguishable color, in part because the only two lamps were fitted with 40 watt bulbs. The shape of the mattress resembled the Bekaar Valley. I could almost hear the lace curtains moan for their former, respectable shade of white. A tray with an electric kettle had a standard issue of four tea bags, one cocoa and two coffee packets, twelve sugars (half brown, half white) and a plastic container with one ounce of "UHT milk", whatever that is. The ever present electric pants press lurked in the corner. In the bathroom, the texture of the towels invited a patent infringement suit from 3M Company's Flexible Abrasives Division. And invariably on the floor lay a scale measuring weight in stones. I checked mine – nearly thirteen stone. What a pleasant thing for British innkeepers to do – relieve us of any concern over how much weight we might gain during our stay by rounding off to the nearest 14 pounds.

I can't fault them for the room sizes. They've convinced me that our ancestors were all shorter than we are and fit in smaller beds and tiny rooms. But my god, you'd think they could hire someone other than a manic-depressive to decorate. Still, we only had to sleep there, not live there.

Breakfast always presents me a treat on my first morning at any of Britain's accommodations. Like all the others, the Original Hotel includes breakfast with the price of the room. "Would you like a cooked breakfast?" the young waitress asked us.

Eileen always declines, deferring to the boxed cereal on the table and some yogurt. Me, I'm a sucker for the Full Scottish Breakfast. Two fried eggs, broiled half tomato, cooked button mushrooms, bangers, two slabs of bacon (the kind with no streaky fat), and on one side black pudding, on the other haggis.

Black pudding or haggis should never be eaten in front of someone with a weak stomach or a hangover. Both are served in a portion about the size of a hockey puck. The pudding, as announced, is black and has the consistency of congealed cream of wheat mixed with rice crispies. It tastes vaguely like gingersnaps soaked in the run-off from slaughtering a steer. That's the better of the two.

Haggis looks more like a mixture of tabouli and tapioca, but has the color of my favorite crayola, burnt umber. (I always wondered what umber was.) It tastes more like fried pork rinds than anything else. I try to forget seeing it in the window of the butcher in Cobham, stuffed bulbous membranes about the size of a softball (my worst fear is that they're pig intestines) with a sign in front, "Haggis, £4.50."

The second morning I always join Eileen for the dry cereal and yogurt.

So on Saturday morning we carried my stomach from the breakfast table to the car and drove the 11 miles into Edinburgh. On short first visits we like to take advantage of the crass, commercial city tour buses. In an hour or so we can learn the city and then go back and revisit what we want to see. In Edinburgh, another reason makes them special. The merchants have achieved staggering success in removing any charm from the first fifteen feet up from street level. The front of almost every building has been ripped from its frame and replaced with glass storefronts. Merchandise, advertising, and signs screaming of despair about stock levels fill the windows. But at fifteen feet and above, the facades of centuries old residences and trade houses remain.

Back to the point of the bus tours. We sat on the top level of the double-decker. We never had to look directly at commercial man's inhumanity to man at the street level.

Even so, pollution has taken its toll in Edinburgh. Like Roslin, many of the buildings were built of local sandstone block. Exhaust fumes from cars and industry had turned the original warm yellow color to a streaked brownish-black. Something like a mixture of black pudding and haggis, I thought, a depressing analogy. Fortuitously, at night the light from the harsh amber street lamps blended pollutant and sandstone into a pleasant straw color, hiding most of the blemish.

Edinburgh Castle has dominated the city for more than eight centuries. Generations of royalty have taken advantage of a 400-foot prehistoric lava mound, located between the city center and the Firth of Forth. Written records show they fortified themselves atop the prominence to consolidate their regional powers as early as the twelfth century.

We followed a tour of the castle led by an impish Scotsman named Stuart Bird. Despite this castle being owned by the British Crown, he took every opportunity to poke his finger in the eye of the English, who were either on the inside or outside during every siege on Edinburgh Castle.

"Ha' many Englishmen du yeh thin' it too' to defen' the gate of the castle?" Stuart Bird asked. He was an expert in Scottish consonant drop. "Five on the draw bridge an' three hunner' on the inside loo'en for the key," he said, his eyes twinkling.

The Scots revere the memory of William Wallace, the man now referred to as Braveheart, who began the war of independence and defeated the English at nearby Stirling Bridge in the thirteenth century. If we believe the Hollywood historians, as his reward shortly after, he was betrayed by his own, drawn and quartered, and shipped in small packages all over the island. Scottish plight was mostly downhill after that, but "Aye laddie," said our guide, "those were the days," before the 700 long years while the insufferable English monarchs reigned.

Stuart Bird could laugh at his own country as well. "How miny of yeh had a Sco'ish brefas' this mornin'? An how miny had haggis?" I was the only one with my hand still up.

"And are you still feeling okay, lad?"

The castle had full view of the Firth (or is it the Forth?) that made Edinburgh an industrial success.

"We still fire the cannon every day at 1 pm to let the ships' quartermasters know the correct time," Stuart Bird told us. "In most other harbors they fire the gun at 12 noon." He lowered his voice to a conspiratorial tone and crinkled his eyes. "But this is Scotland, so we save eleven rounds each day."

As at Buckingham and Windsor, a full time military detachment remains assigned to Edinburgh to preserve the romantic image. Young soldiers in ceremonial dress kilts manned the portals. Their main function seemed to be posing while tourists photograph each other next to them, documenting the wonderful time they were having. I snapped two of Eileen.

"You know what a Scotsman wears under his kilt, I suppose," Steward Bird asked the crowd. "I'll tell you a wee secret. How many of you are going to the Tattoo tonight? At the end you'll see the lone piper in the spotlight atop the castle wall. They had to put lead weights at the bottom of his kilt. Otherwise, if it's windy, he'd shock the faint heart of many a fair lass in the audience."

Stuart Bird wore a beautiful pair of blue tartan trousers. A little later on the tour I asked him, "Almost all the military I see here are wearing kilts. How come you wear pants?"

With another twinkle, he answered, "I canna find a kilt long enough."

Later that night we returned to the castle. When we had received confirmation of our hotel room on Tuesday, the tourist bureau sent us a "What's going on in Edinburgh this year" pamphlet. I just happened to notice that the Military Tattoo started this weekend.

"Why don't you call and get tickets," I had asked Eileen casually.

And she did. We hadn't a clue how lucky we were until we saw the "sold out" sign at the ticket office that night when we picked up ours. Dejected looking tourists milled about the area asking for scalped tickets because the Military Tattoo is to Edinburgh what Rodeo is to Houston, Stampede is to Calgary, and Rex's Parade is to Mardi Gras – the main event.

Fending off the poor devils, we joined the 39,998 others tramping up the steep back streets to our seats around the parade ground at the castle entrance. On the cue of the loudspeaker, the crowd went silent, the lights went out, and gas torches fired up along the castle gate. Hidden lighting drenched the castle walls in blood red color. The booming voice of the master of ceremonies announced something, but I only recognized four words, "Royal Scottish Marching Highlanders."

Across the castle drawbridge marched a single figure, outfitted in tartan and kilt of bright red, green, and navy. His military strut left no doubt his rank was Sergeant Major. We watched him turn in the spotlight, pound his massive staff on the planks three times, and bark commands in strange tongue. The night filled with the sound of three dozen bagpipes and just as many brass and percussion. In perfect cadence 72 military bandsmen in the same richly colored uniforms followed their leader's footsteps across the drawbridge and then performed precision maneuvers up and down the grounds. For the next 15 minutes, the music, the lighting, the choreographed marching, and the barrage of inconceivably brilliant colors captivated us. Who would think we could stand to listen to bagpipes for the next hour and a half?

Other groups followed the Highlanders. The Gurkas from Pakistan were a spectacle. Sword-flailing dancers in costumes of white linen performed to Pakistani melodies played on bagpipes by brown men in forest green tartan. A huge black *major domo*, shouting commands that would cow a Green Beret, led the Trinidad and Tobago Marching Band out of the castle. They played a pugnacious march on their steel drums until they reached the center point of the arena. At the drop of his baton, a metamorphosis took place as the band broke into a calypso version of a Scottish folk song. The stiff-necked pretension of the *major domo* melted into an undulating high step. The band members bumped and cavorted, creating ten minutes of Carnivale Edinburgh.

In another ten-minute interlude, a team from the Scottish Special Forces simulated the defense of the castle against a team of would-be terrorists. The Scots repelled down the castle walls and advanced, firing their automatic assault weapons. I would have written this episode off as inane if they hadn't made fun of themselves at the end. Just as the terrorists seemed to prevail, a Mel Gibson look-alike with blue-painted face stripes, tartan flung over his shoulder and sword in hand trapezed to the middle of the parade ground. As he beat the intruders back, the announcer bellowed, "Once again, Braveheart saves Scottish honor. "

That set up the next assault – on the emotional Scottish patriotism evident to us all day. "Ladies and gentlemen, it has been 25 years since the Scottish Highlanders reached the top of the popular charts with this next piece. Brace yourselves for their rendition of 'Amazing Grace.'" And how sweet it was to hear those refrains, familiar in melody and words, but in a haunting setting. The crowd's exhilaration grew palpably.

The entire troupe of performers then assembled on the parade ground. 72 bagpipes and 128 accompanying instruments began "Brave Scotland." Everyone in the outside world knows that melody but almost no one knows the name. There was no doubt in my mind what that song meant to the people around the parade ground as they held each others hands and swayed. I could feel the music stirring the soul of nationalism. If someone had jumped onto center stage and ordered a march on Westminster, thirty thousand souls would have jumped up in support and demanded of the British Parliament that very night, "Devolution be damned. Independence now!"

I think the final touch was meant for riot control. At the end of "Brave Scotland," the lights blinked off. The gas torches died. A spotlight played on a single piper atop the ramparts. I listened to the sucking sound of chests expanding as his pipes moaned the Scottish version of "Taps."

A magnificent fireworks display, accompanied music in syncopated time by the ensemble, finished off the night. Forty thousand spectators poured into the single narrow street leading from the castle. I had visions of bulls stampeding through the streets of Pamplona, but the crowd behaved and we reached our car in a few minutes. Eileen and I agreed we wouldn't tell a soul what we had experienced. If the word got out, we'd never be able to get a ticket for next year's show.

****

Five weeks later Scotland celebrated the 700th anniversary of William "Braveheart" Wallace's victory at the River Forth, upstream of the Firth. That night we watched on television as the citizens of Scotland voted by a three to one margin to establish a Scottish Parliament and the beginnings of Home Rule. The debate leading to the vote had introduced a new word into the popular lexicon, *devolution*, the delegation of power from the central government to local rule. With ratification by the British Parliament, decision-making began migration from London back to Edinburgh and its elected Scottish officials, making it even more imprudent to call a Scot a Brit.

Bill Leffler

August 18

Dear Richard,

The tourists have overrun the country. Our kids just left yesterday. What a zoo. Two days before his arrival date Middle Kid called and said he had lost his passport and would be a day late getting here. Youngest Kid arrived direct from college with a suitcase full of dirty clothes for Mom to wash. Oldest Kid said he only brought three days of clean clothes. That morning our tiny, frontloading washing machine had broken with the door in the closed position. All, I mean all, Bill's underwear was in there and he had to wear a pair of mine while he drove us to the airport. He went especially slow so as to not have an accident and have to go to hospital. Meanwhile the repairman came and Youngest and Oldest ran around the kitchen trying to make him tea but forgot to put any water in the electric kettle and burned out the coil.

This being the eighth wave of visitors since May, I've fallen into just pushing them out of the car two miles from here at Hampton Court Palace the first day and telling them I'll pick them up in three hours. But a trip to London is another thing. I have to escort them. After eight times I can tell exactly where the Royal Polishers missed the tarnish on the Crown Jewels. And I wonder if the Guards are as unspeakably jaded as I am when they do their Changing every day. One thing I never get tired of, though, is Prime Minister's day before the House of Commons. (I am now on a first name basis with our local MP's secretary so I can get tickets at will.) The Loyal Opposition is appallingly unruly when the Minister speaks, rolling their eyes, moaning, and guffawing at his remarks. They even get up and shake their fingers across the chamber at the Government members, but always remembering not to cross the green line in front of their benches, a sword's length from the line on the opposite side. It's called "toeing the line," I've heard from the guide eight times now.

As a treat for my guests, I went to Claygate for scones last week. It was before nine and it wasn't Monday, baker's day off, so I was sure I was safe. Would you believe it: no scones or any baked goods? "Where are they," I almost shouted at the counter lady. "Oh sorry, it's baker's two week holiday. Nothing until next Tuesday." Rrrrr.

TJDGI #5: A bill arrived from the Town Council for our television license. £96 for the year gives us the privilege of turning on our TV whenever we want. And this quote from the bill: "If you are registered blind and present your local authority certificate, you may pay £1.25 less."

Love, your frazzled sister

8

Yo, Shakespeare!

All our prospective visitors from America, having suddenly become our new pen pals, had been asking, "Have you been to the Globe? It's supposed to be an exact replica of the theater where Shakespeare premiered his plays."

Elizabethan plays in a theater designed four hundred years ago. Not high our list. We are not Shakespeare fans. We found him hard to understand when the nuns made us read him in high school. It always puzzled me how he made a living as a playwright. Could seventeenth century playgoers really understand what the plots were all about? Could they follow the dialogue? Were they more sophisticated than we are? And if so, why did they wear those white knee socks after Labor Day?

I can count on one hand how many Shakespeare plays we have seen. Almost every time we went, we had some reason in mind that would have caused my English Lit professor severe depression. We went to *Midsummer Night's Dream* in Stratford-on-Avon twenty years ago because that's what you do when you visit the Bard's hometown. We went to *Taming of the Shrew* at the Winedale Festival two years ago as a ruse for four couples to play golf in the hills of Central Texas before and after. And so on. Literati we ain't.

So now came our son's best friend, David, to Surrey for the first leg of his post-graduate Grand Tour. Nowadays, Grand Tour means bumming a bed and a few meals from as many of your parent's friends stationed in Europe as you can contact and staying in youth hostels and eating soup and French bread the rest of the time. David had taken up acting in Shakespearean productions in his senior year at the University of Texas, and played the husband in *Shrew* last spring at Winedale. His only request of us, weeks before he arrived: "Could you get us tickets for a performance at the Globe?"

The Globe sits on its original site, they tell us, next to the River Thames but in a backwater part of London. A nearby tube stop, Mansion House, meant only a five minute walk across Thames on the Southwark Bridge, one of fifteen crossings we could choose from between Hammersmith to the west and Gravesend to the east. Actually we could choose from only fourteen. Prolific as they have been over the centuries, London bridge builders have recently fallen off the learning curve. Authorities deemed the newest, the Millennium Bridge, unsafe for traffic three days after it opened in 2000, as it swayed precariously in the summer breezes.

As we crossed the Southwark, a double-decker bus passed us. The register above the driver's window read "Sorry – out of service." The British are disproportionately apologetic in almost every aspect of life. They will say sorry if they sneeze, if they can't hear what you said, or if you're riding the underground and smash their ribs in a sudden start. In fact the only time you won't hear "sorry" is if they have to accept blame for some blunderously incompetent mistake, like building the Millennium Bridge or returning the wrong change.

After the river crossing we wandered for another ten minutes through the narrow streets of the Bankside and Bear Gate neighborhoods. All were festooned with empty potato crisp bags, Mars wrappers, Evian bottles, and other contemporary detritus. Shabby homes were mixed with dismal office fronts. I half expected to see Bob Kratchit carrying Tim home on his shoulder.

A sandwich board sign on the sidewalk in front of the theater announced ominously.

A WINTER'S TALE
TICKETS AS LOW AS £4.50.

I looked at our tickets. Twelve pounds fifty each. Hmmm. At the bottom, the ticket gave a curious message:

ALL STAR CASTE
GOOD FOR ONE PERFORMANCE ONLY

I hoped it was tonight's.

Just inside the theater, a gnomic fellow hawking cushions intercepted us. I always get apprehensive when I see someone renting cushions near the doorway to a theater or stadium. They are giving me this forewarning: "This place is so uncomfortable, I can make a living renting cushions for one pound fifty each." I never resist. I always rent cushions.

Despite its triumph in authenticity, the seating in the Globe wouldn't even qualify as bleachers in an

American stadium. It approaches something more like a Little League field, where only parents tolerate pine board benches with no backs. We thought ourselves lucky that we had last row seats with a wooden bulkhead behind us. Wrong. It took just five minutes to find out why chairs don't have backs perpendicular to the seats. People don't sit at right angles. Chair backs are supposed to slope. Even my foresight at renting cushions aggravated the situation. With the extra two-inch boost, Eileen could see well, but her feet didn't reach the floor. Before the lights dimmed, her legs went to sleep

The open-air stage at the Globe sits about five feet above the floor level. In front lay a large courtyard where the four pound fifty ticket holders, about sixty of them that night, were entitled to stand for the whole performance. Behind them were the stalls with their wooden benches where we sat, circling the courtyard about twenty feet up. The only people in the theater who looked comfortable sat in the Royal Boxes at either end of the semi-circle. Coat and tie gentlemen and ladies in lemon-colored suits relaxed in real chairs. Attendants in black livery served them cucumber sandwiches and Pimm's Cups in tall glasses throughout the performance. We could almost hear the chatter, "Splendid, Godfrey. That's enough" or "more gin, my dear?"

So here was the scene: one set of spectators stood in the courtyard, already shifting from one foot to another, leaning on their partners, rubbing their necks, stiff from looking up at the stage. The rest of us squirmed on hard benches or sat numb-legged on cushions. This theater company has to be good, I thought, for all these people to tolerate this aggravation.

On the way in, Eileen had asked an attendant if the playbill (which cost two pounds) gave a synopsis of the plot. "Well no, dear," she blew her off. "We've all read it in school."

Luckily David had worked his way into a copy of the play he had brought from Austin. "It's not too complicated. Two Italian princes who are, like, brothers, you know, and one of them accuses his new wife of infidelity with the other, you know, and has her executed, you know, but she has a baby first, you know, and the newborn daughter gets spirited away or something, you know, and a farmer finds her and he has this son, you know, who eventually falls in love with her, but he betrays the first Prince's aide … But I'm only up to the fourth act. There are four more after that."

Eight acts. This could be a long night, I thought. You know?

The play began. Eileen had already given up her seat and moved down four rows to an empty front bench where she could slump onto the railing and lean her chin on her forearms. With her gone, I could slouch sideways on my pine two-by-eight, alternating my cheeks. On to the stage marched two corpulent Henry VIII look-a-likes, one even larger than the other. A motley retinue in seventeenth century drag followed.

"How frun dust lents mor shummeth?" the larger of the two Henrys asked.

The other responded, with much hand shaking and laughter amongst all, "We smee poff noneth win flebble."

Now I'm like most other post-middle aged men. I have trouble hearing most stage dialogue, no less oratory with a British accent. But I figure that if I can catch about forty percent, I have a chance of enjoying the play.

Leering at the large bosomed woman standing between them, Henry the Lesser asks Henry the Greater, "When will Cleavigina offal sur lebration? Mill torsley parsley farsley?"

"Milord! Wuff nost be fluffer an fluffer?"

"Nost aye. Moost yeah?"

Well so far I was getting about twelve percent, so I decided I needed to watch this like a foreign movie with subtitles, except I can't see the subtitles. Once I made this mental adjustment, *A Winter's Tale* became an ensemble of mimes. Dialogue became irrelevant. Their performance moved me from celebration and marital bliss to anxiety, suspicion, rage, repentance, new love, triumph, and ecstasy. What more could I ask for from Shakespeare?

Evidently, even the real fans needed a break from the heavy wordage. Somewhere in the second or fourth act – no way to tell – a boisterous voice emerged from under our stalls. A character dressed in a trenchcoat and gangster hat and sporting sunglasses swaggered up to the stage like the ghost of Mickey Spillane. "Yo, Thalidomidicus," he bellowed. "Whilst we conaff or shanazee, wouldst thou frenzle thine lobotomous?"

Raucous laughter rolled through the audience. This was, no doubt, the comedic climax of the play.

Mickey reappeared on stage sporadically throughout the remaining two or three acts of the play. I suppose the director wanted to create a post-modern

112

Greek chorus. Or maybe he owed the guy a large sum of money. At the finale, Mickey reappeared, without trenchcoat and hat, still with sunglasses, but in baggy knee-lengths and a T-shirt that announced "UMBRO." He mugged his bow well enough to get a big hand, even from the exhausted gallery of standees in the courtyard.

On our train ride home, I asked David and Eileen, "What did you think?"

"That was great," said David. "I mean, a lot funner than I thought. Thanks for getting the tickets."

Funner, I thought. This is from my son's friend, the Shakespearean actor? Fun, funner, funnest. I suppose that's how we all got from the way Bill S. wrote four hundred years ago to what we speak today. I was going to make this profound observation to Eileen, but I noticed she had already fallen asleep.

"Great story," said David. "I mean, great story, you know?"

September 13

Dear Richard,

We took a country walk with Stephanie and Alistair on Sunday. Britain is covered with a web of public footpaths. The local landowners get a small stipend from the government to maintain them. Stephanie brought a book, "Pub Walks in Surrey." She told us we must have unconditional and enduring faith to use it. For example, "...continue straightaway, with the hillock to your right, crossing a trail near a large Scots pine..." and "Pass a sign on a Welsh fir that says NO HORSES and turn left." My favorite was "Turn in at the grit box near the base of a steep hill." If we didn't know a Scots pine from a Welsh fir, we'd still be roaming the Downs. But these guides are always correct and dependable. How very British. The best part of the walk, of course, is the pub at the end. A cool (not cold) glass of lager and a steak and kidney pie is enough to finish you off for the rest of the afternoon.

On the walk we came across a small stone church build by the Normans in the twelfth century and still in use. It has a list of all the parish priests and vicars back to the beginning, so long ago they didn't have last names. The engraving over the entrance said, "This is the Gate to Heaven. Enter thee by this door." Underneath someone had taped a neatly written note, "This entrance is locked on account of the draft. Please use the side door."

TJDGI #6: Kelly told me she went to the supermarket to get potato chips for her kid's high school outing. She brought a bunch of bags to the checkout. The elderly checker, apparently still psychopathically stressed by the shortages during WW ll, blanched as she counted the bags. "You have eighteen here. Have you left none for anyone else?" Kelly looked at her. "Eighteen? Hmm. Just a minute." She went across the aisle and got the last two bags from the shelf and tossed them on the checkout counter. "I guess I hadn't," she said.

I didn't know whether I was going to be able to finish out the tennis season. I developed a bad case of tennis elbow. Probably because tennis balls are so expensive here, people rarely break out a fresh can. They just go over to the pro's bin and pick out a couple of used. Well with all the rain, they weigh a ton and that's likely what has been doing in my elbow. "Go for physio," Lulu told me. "Everyone does." So I tried it. The therapist worked wonders. No cortisone shots, no pills. Just rubbing, massaging, and continuous chatter. Magic. I feel better already. Maybe she's one of those sorceresses from Glastonbury. Who cares? And I've put out the word to our prospective houseguests – a few fresh cans of tennis balls make a nice gift.

Love, your mending sister

9

Munro

"So, whe' a' ya stayin'?" John Russell asked us.

"At the Maryculter Hotel in the Peterculter section of Aberdeen."

"Oh, ya mean the Marycoota in Petercoota. Aye, it's a wee place but nice. They say the Knights Templar built it in 1255."

Eileen stage-whispered to me, "I hope they've changed out the mattresses since."

In a louder voice she asked John, "I read in some magazine that the Knights Templar were what we call mercenaries today. They were a secret society of thugs that would hire out to whatever local despot offered them the most money. Didn't they run the local vigilantes for the manor lords here when they went off to the Holy Land crusades?"

John tucked his chin into his neck. "Well, I doah' know abou' tha.' An' I sugges' you doah' bring it up in the Templar Bar in the Marycoota."

John had invited about twenty of us to join him for a hike in the Scottish Highlands one weekend in October. "It'll be just a' easy stroll because we take along the women and children and the dog. When we're done we can have lunch and a pint or two at the local pub. And we might get my neighbor Fiobhan to give us a tour of the whiskey distillery nearby."

Our limited stay in Edinburgh had passed far too quickly, so on Saturday we hopped a British Air flight for the hundred minute trip to the land of the long shadows. Aberdeen sits almost at the tip of Britain. That puts it at higher latitude than Newfoundland and parallel to Juneau, Alaska. If it weren't for the Gulf Steam bringing the warm waters of the Caribbean right past, the whole area would be under snow a good part the year. As it was, daylight hours of October lasted only from eight to five as the sun traversed the sky just above the southern hilltops.

So in the middle of the night we rose to make our rendezvous with the intrepid John Russell and friends at nine. The night before I had asked the Maryculter receptionist if we could get breakfast before we left. "We serve a full Scottish breakfast starting at eight on Sunday," she offered.

"Well, we have to leave here about seven. Is there a place around that serves breakfast that early?"

She sucked a small chin into her long neck, which I began to think was a local affliction. "Another place that serves breakfast? No, people have their breakfast here."

"No cafe's or restaurants like Denny's or Big Boy's?"

"Well, I doah' know abou' that." (They doah' seem to want to say 'no' in this country.) "Bu' I can leave you a breakfast in your room tonight."

The next morning we had our choice of coffee or tea and Choco-Pops or Weetabix, a substance that looked suspiciously like dried haggis. The pitcher of heavy cream that accompanied the cereal did not have the slightest hint of turning, despite sitting on the dresser all night. I suppose that had to do with them turning off the heat at about eleven with the temperature in the room dropping to about ten degrees centigrade.

About sixty minutes south of Aberdeen we turned off the coast road and drove through a parade of villages and hamlets just below thick, cloying fog. Each cluster of homes was a clone of the last – gray granite construction, lace-curtained windows, and small flower gardens in the front. The gloomy light that penetrated the mist showed no sign of life except an occasional wisp of chimney smoke. In the dimness we saw that the road paralleled a river meandering down the center of a deepening valley. The road, for the most part, abutted the southside hills while the river made a serpentine trace down the valley floor. The ribbon of gray water had no banks, just water abutting green grass. The unbroken valley bottom had no natural obstacles and no obvious reason why the river shouldn't take the direct route toward the sea. For that matter, another inch or two of rain and the whole valley floor would probably be under water. We could understand why the roadside houses clung to the rising hills.

We followed the river for fifteen miles up the valley, having put complete faith in the one sign at the turn-off that assured us "Glen Clova 15." We really had no choice but to trust the cardinal rule of signposting in Great Britain – when it's time to turn, the signposts will tell you to turn; until then, come roundabout or junction, don't turn. Still, fifteen miles with crossroads and turn-offs sorely tested our commitment. Our map proved useless. Not one of the settlements we drove through announced a name to reassure us. Either they were too small to warrant one or too tight with their purses to erect a sign. This *was* Scotland.

In the larger villages, we did see signs for that ubiquitous accommodation to personal distress, "TOILETS." The people of this island are obsessed with public convenience. Someday I will have to trace the origins of the civic commitment to the retail end of human waste disposal. Wherever a hundred people congregate, the government follows quickly behind with the construction of a concrete excretorium and scattered signposts directing the discomforted traveler. Of course, in contrast to America, there are no Denny's or Big Boys here, or even local cafes to offer free enterprise facilities. But even in the larger towns and cities where commercial establishments abound, the municipal amenities lurk nearby. And the inventor of the water closet, the nineteenth century Royal Sanitary Engineer, Thomas Crapper, is to Britain what Johnny Appleseed is to America.

Actually, "toilet" is one of several words used unabashedly in Britain but is shunned in America. I can never remember hearing anyone back home say to a hostess, "Could you tell me where the toilet is?" They would have gotten a puzzled look and response, "Why, it's in the bathroom." And while I'm on the subject, another is *underpants*. Real men in America don't say *underpants*. They say *shorts* or *skivvies*. But just the other day I had a consultant tell me that we should get so close to our competitors they'll find us in their underpants.

Almost at the moment of despair, the road ended abruptly at a gateway marked Glen Clova Recreational Area. Beyond, thirty or forty cars crowded around a gray blockhouse marked "TOILETS." We recognized our group on the fringe and joined them.

Open trunks and car doors displayed a colorful assortment of gear. The members of our crew of twenty were pulling on heavy woolen socks, hiking boots, hi- and low-tech rain suits in plain green or electric blue and Alpine yellow. Our dashing organizer, John Russell, stomped back and forth, prodding and herding. He wore a Glengary atop his head, a traditional wax jacket, what my father called knickers but he called plus-fours (so-called because they fall four inches below the kneecaps), olive knee socks with red tassels at the top, and green wellies. He regaled in his authenticity.

Hans Bakker, our young Dutch friend was calibrating his hand held satellite tracker. "Ja, we joost read of this ordinance map our actual coordinates. Den when we are anywhere, we can tell where we are by reading the new coordinates what the satellite delivers us."

The notion that we might need such assistance made my stomach vaguely uneasy – or maybe the heavy cream was starting to turn. But we would not have the rest of them thinking we had just fallen off the pumpkin wagon as it passed by the car park. So donned our own rain jackets, threw our UT Longhorn sweatshirts into our knapsacks, and smartly joined the column as it headed into the forest. Deflating any signs of smugness the two of us might have had, Hans pulled a metal cylinder from his upper arm pocket, snapped it into a five-foot, telescoping, magnesium-alloy, walking stick and fell in behind us.

Two hundred paces into the trees we gathered around a large bulletin board that offered us the option of a dozen destinations and routes. John Russell studied them uneasily, hand on chin. "He's probably trying to figure out the easiest path today, what with yesterday's rain and all," I said to Eileen.

"Sure."

Off we marched again. I stayed up with John and asked him, "Tell me again. How long is this hike?"

"Oh, just a wee amble, really. Maybe six or seven miles, but half of it is coming down the munro, so that doesn't count, does it?"

"Down the munro…?"

"Aye, the munro. That's what we'll be climbing, the munro at the head of the glen."

He looked at the furrows in my brows. "You doah' know what a munro is, do ya? We only have one mountain here in Scotland. Called Ben Nevis. But the rest are too small to be mountains, too big to be hills. Munros."

Too small to be mountains, I thought to myself. That sounds okay. But still, if half the six mile hike is coming down, the first three miles must be …

We slogged through the muddy woods along a tumbling mountain stream that reminded us we were moving rapidly uphill. After an hour we abruptly stepped out of the trees to a brilliant vista of green. A huge bowl scooped from the munro that lay in front of us. Not a tree stood between us and the top, but the entire face lay covered with lush, long-bladed grass that rippled invitingly in the breeze. A narrow ribbon of water spilled over the top of the bowl, eventually wending its way past us and disappearing into the woods.

"John, how far is it up to that waterfall?" Eileen asked him breathlessly as she caught up.

"To the top of Fee Burn? About an hour."

"Fee what?"

"Fee Burn. That slip of water is called a burn," and for the second time John burred the r in Burn like a wooden spoon on a washboard. 'And that's Fee Burn there in front of us on it's way to becoming the River Esk in the middle of the Glen. But I doah' know who Burn was."

"What's the source of that water on the top? Is there a plateau?"

"Oh no. There's another munro or two beyond that you canna' see from here. But you will when we get there."

Everyone else in the party seemed to know that snack time had arrived because they had opened their rucksacks and unloaded thermoses of coffee, fruit, sandwiches, and granola bars. Eileen and I had already eaten the two Mars Bars I had picked up at a petrol station earlier and we were hoarding the two bottles of fizzy water we had filched from the Maryculter. Whatever happened to lunch at the pub? What's all this early sustenance and what does everyone know that we don't?

A kindly colleague offered us some steaming hot coffee spiked with brandy, and it went down quicker than the falls atop Fee Burn.

"Ready? Onwards mates," cried John Russell, and the young bucks of the group bounded toward the bowl. Hans checked his satellite position and confirmed, "Ja, ve are right here," and left. Ominously, a family of four, including two pre-teen daughters, decided to stick to the lowlands. Eileen and I watched them wistfully as they made their excuses and retreated into the woods.

With deep breaths we headed into the grassy canyon. The path along Fee Burn quickly became vague and the trajectory turned decidedly upward. The vanguard of our group became less easy to distinguish as they bounded forward. Our casual gait gave way to deliberate footfalls and hand over fist climbing around grassy moguls. We used clumps of the strong-bladed grass as handholds to pull ourselves around rocks and scree. The waterfall was not the only source for Fee Burn. Water leaked from countless hidden sources below the grass and ran in rivulets toward the stream. Our woolen stocks squished in our boots.

In a half-hour the older and less hardy stopped with us to rest every five minutes. As we approached the top, I found myself humming desperately,

> *The bear went over the munro*
> *The bear went over the munro ...*

I was afraid to find out what he saw when he got there.

Just as we approached our moment of triumph, the top of the burn, the sky closed in on us. A dark gray cloud swept around the rim of the bowl. Visibility dropped to a few meters. Gusty winds knocked us on our butts in the grass. Freezing rain pelted our faces, the only exposed parts of our bodies, but making us feel totally wet outside and in. "All those that are having fun, would you raise your hands?" shouted John Russell as he scrambled back down the slope to encourage us.

The squall lasted only six minutes, but the thick cloud remained nearly within reach when we stood at the crest. We looked back down the bowl and could barely trace the burn to our departure point where the burn entered the forest. In my state of near delirium I imagined standing at a Baskin-Robbins counter gazing into a half-empty container of mint ice cream with chocolate syrup running down to the center.

In a moment of compassion John Russell shouted to us above the wind, "We're running a wee bit late. I think we'll not have time to go the next two munro before we start down. We'll just traverse the top of the bowl and start down the east side."

I wondered if he tried hard to have an r-word in every sentence he said so that he can run the spoon along the washboard. No matter. I would probably kill this labially-challenged dolt anyway when we reached the bottom.

By practicing our exhausted and pathetic looks, we elicited more hot coffee and snacks of sunflower seeds, fresh parsnip sticks, and a half sandwich of prawn mayonnaise and salmon. My God, we were desperate.

As we stumbled along the rim, the clouds momentarily opened and we gaped at the rolling surf of munros to our right, each with its own furious waterfall made violent by the cloudbursts. Ahead, down the eastern slope, we saw verdant valleys a thousand feet below, filled with Christmas tree forests.

We lurched downward with desperate urgency. More squalls assailed us, one with driven sleet.

Six hours after we started, we rejoined the vanguard and the deserters at the car park. In a moment of engineering triumph, Hans checked his coordinates for the last time. "See. Vee are back again vhere vee ver."

As we stripped off our rain gear and wet socks, John Russell appealed to us. "We are supposed to go for a pint and lunch now, but we need to go directly to the distillery. Fiobhan's waiting on her Sunday off to give us the private tour."

Bordering on insurrection, we dragged our sodden bodies into our cars and drove half way down Glen Clova, back to the foothills of the Scottish Highlands.

The village of Fettercairn takes its name from the stone prominence that overlooks it. The Gaelic *fetter* means *in front of,* John Russell had told us. A *cairn* can be anything from a pile of stones marking a gravesite to a large stone hill. The Scots use *cairn* almost as loosely as the English use *pudding* (*Yorkshire pudding,* a light pastry accouterment to roast beef; *steak and kidney pudding,* a puff pastry-topped pot pie; *summer pudding,* a mixture of fruit, meal, and syrup; or generally anything sweet served for dessert, as in *"Care for some pud', luv?"* But not the chocolate stuff served in America, which the Brits call custard.)

Not many human emotions are more intense than Scottish pride in whiskey. It ranks higher on their list than Harris Tweed and just below kilts and tartan. Great Britain allows the Bank of Scotland to issue its own legal tender and the Scottish ten pound note has

Sir Walter Scott on its face and on its reverse a whiskey distillery. The equivalent to Alexander Hamilton and the U.S. Treasury on his backside, I suppose.

A nice, but totally unintelligible lady welcomed us to the unassuming tourist facilities at the Fettercairn Distillery. For a few minutes I thought she was speaking Gaelic. "Ah lik a welcaya to Fettercairn an hoo ya ha an ineresin time ..."

She retired to the projection room and left us to a slide show extolling the virtues of single malt whiskey. Luckily the narration had subtitles. As we watched the *ineresin* show, I thought surely now I would have the chance to find out what single malt whiskey is, without giving the appearance of a complete simpleton.

Our hostess returned with a tray of small square glasses with a golden liquid in them. "A wee dram mi be dough and afta noo or carr," she said, and everyone shook their heads in vague agreement, took one, and sipped it. In a few minutes she led us into the distillery, past water settling tanks, big copper stills, and barrel filling stations. We recoiled on cue when she opened the two fermenting tanks. Out came noxious vapors, bubbling from a bilious brew resembling the effluent from a Roman vomitorium. "Nees abih more fermenin," she said pensively.

As we moved through a complex of pipes and gauges, I finally blurted out, "But why is this called a *single malt* whiskey?"

You'd have thought I just said Rob Roy was a sissy because he wore a kilt all the time. Fiobhan took a moment to relax her eyebrows and compose herself and answered what I interpreted to be "It's because it's whiskey from a single malt. Not a wee bit of anything else. Just a single malt."

Nineteen heads turned from her to me in a moment of dramatic pause. "That's the dumbest bit of tautological crap I've ever heard," lay on the edge of my lips as my tongue touched my front teeth. But in a moment of discretion my lips re-formed into a circle, my head started bobbing, and I heard myself say, "Ooh. Uh huh," and we turned and followed her to the storehouse where barrels of Old Fettercairn single malt lay aging in the cool quiet.

Later, I found out from our fellow hikers that more than ninety percent of the Scotch whiskeys we drink in America are combinations of stocks made from various malts, blended to an acceptable taste. Scores of small distilleries like Fettercairn use exceptional and costly processing so that their whiskey, made from a single source of malt, is drinkable. That's why single malts sell at a big premium. Fettercairn must be on the borderline. They sell some by the bottle, but nearly ninety percent of their output goes to other distillers for blending, though I didn't have enough of that wee dram in the square glass to tell why.

"Onward people," John Russell cried. "Dinner awaits us at the Inn."

John had booked us into the finest restaurant in Fettercairn. That may bring a smile to your face, but this little town had a reputation for fine dining. However, it's not likely that our presence that night did anything to enhance their fame.

Eileen and I lingered at the back as John Russell made his way into the Inn. After a few moments we followed the queue through the door. We passed the hostess who had a frozen, tight-lipped smile on her lips but horror in her eyes. She had just seen tramp before her a ratty crew of twenty that looked like they could have slept under the eaves of Waterloo Station the night before. As a concession to decency, most of us had taken off our hiking boots, but even so we were a spectacle – sweaty, wild-haired, and mud-spattered from the waists down.

In the dining room, the other patrons stared, aghast with their hands over their mouths or clutching their chests as we, in our anoraks and knit caps, seated ourselves at our white-linened and candled tables. For the next hour we explored the merits of Old Fettercairn in detail, glass by square glass. Eventually, with typically insufferable manner, the waitstaff plied us with cold salmon from the local rivers, wild mushrooms from the forests, Angus sirloins, and endless bottles of Nouveau Beaujolais. Assuring us safeguard from mad cow disease, the menu tracked the pedigree of the beef to individually registered steers on local farms.

All of this disappeared in what seemed a matter of minutes as everyone frantically replaced the carbs and calories expended on the munros of Glen Clova.

Watching Brits and Scots eat is a study in efficiency. They all keep their knives in their right hands and forks in their left, with none of the awkward shuffle that Americans do – cutting, disengaging, putting down the knife, changing the fork to the other hand, re-forking, and transporting. Brits just cut and stuff. Some of them cut, layer, and stuff – piling the potatoes, two or three vegetables, and gravy on top of the speared meat to create a well balanced meal on every forkful. Altogether, a remarkable display of productivity.

I asked my buddy, Henry, one time why he thought the Brits ate with the round side of the fork up when it was obviously designed for the hollow side up. "You don't use a spoon upside down," I pointed out to him.

"Goes back to big families and small dining rooms," he said. "If I tried to pile food on the hollow side with my knife, I'd have to stick both my elbows out and I'd poke the persons next to me. Hollow side down I can just prong the meat and pile on the accompaniments." He had a only a half grin as he looked me in the eye. I couldn't tell if he was kidding or not, so I tried another on him.

"Well how come your salt shakers only have one hole while the pepper shakers have five or six? That's backwards too."

"When I was a lad," Henry said, "it was common for us to pile salt on the corner of our plates and dip our food into it as we ate. It was easy to do with the fork pointing down with all the food on it. So we needed just a solitary hole in our saltcellars to make a mound."

They are so unbearably orderly when they eat.

"Ready for sweets, are you?" the waitress asked the tousled twenty. Waitresses always ask this question with naughty voices and coy smiles on their faces, as if we were about to commit a venial sin together. Out came large bowls of Golden Syrup Sponge Pudding with Custard, along with pitchers of heavy cream to be poured on top. Trays of Scottish cheeses, oatcakes, grapes, and walnuts followed. In the warm afterglow, a fulfilled feeling overtook me. Despite the exhausting hike on the munros, the day had left me with no shortages of triglycerides or cholesterol.

On our flight home, British Airways generously served Eileen and I each a small bottle of Glenfidditch single malt whiskey. "To John Russell, damn his eyes," we toasted with clinked glasses, savoring the peaty aroma that drifted out of our throats as we swallowed the amber liquid.

"The Scots. They're like their whiskey, you know."

"How's that?"

"Hardy. Usually drunk before supper. And they don't make anything like it in England."

Bill Leffler

October 5

Dear Richard,

Never get sick in Britain. Bill came home with a massive back spasm that laid him out on the den floor for five days. We finally got him to an orthopaedic surgeon, Mr. Solemn on Harley Street in London. I gather that's the equivalent of a Park Avenue doctor. After looking at Bill's MRI he gave his learned opinion. "I'm afraid, old man, that your backbone's just worn out. I should think you'd take some physio and learn to live with it." He blew off that Bill couldn't lift his left foot off the ground and walked like Quasimoto. Then we went to Mr. Johnson, a neurosurgeon who was anxious to cut. So we "went to hospital" and let him, reluctantly. Lucky for us private health care here is ten steps ahead of the National Health Service. A friend of ours with a rotator cuff tear had to wait 15 weeks just to see a NHS surgeon. Anyway, we went to this nice hospital where a solicitous concierge took us to a private room. The surgery went well, but during his only post-op visit, Mr. Johnson said, "Home tomorrow. Peek under the bandage next week and see if there's a gap. If not, just snip the stitches a week later. I'll see you in three months." And he left. The sister (nurse) with him said on her way out the door, "That's all. We'll send all the papers to your home." No help, no instructions, no wheel chair to take Bill out to the car. They're all obliging and grins on the way in, but just "toodle-lu, old man" on the way out. Never get sick in Britain.

Lulu, who you remember is only about half my age, invited us for dinner at her Cobham cottage. Her husband, James, stared at us all evening. We found out later that when she explained to him who we were, he asked her, "Do they have children?" "Yes, they're our age." Lulu told us later that he couldn't figure out how we could look so old for people in their late twenties.

At dinner Lulu announced we were having lamb roast and that she had gone to her parent's estate just that morning and picked out the lamb for slaughter. I didn't want to think about it too much. As she offered it to Bill, she said, "And we have lots more gravy." Lulu looked "gobsmacked" when Old Wax-in-the-Ears asked her if Lotsmore gravy was a local recipe.

TJDGI #7: Brits love queues. (The saying goes, put three Brits anywhere in the world and they'll form a queue.) In the supermarket the other day, in front of the checkout that has the sign, "baskets only," six women with baskets on their arms stood in the queue. Further down there were four wider-aisled checkouts for trolleys, all empty.

TJDGI #8: Scotland has the highest incidence of heart disease in the country. We drove through the town of Dundee and in one of the many fish and chips shops, we saw a sign, "The Perfect Sweet: Battered and Deep-fried Mars Bars."

Lulu and I came in third in the All-Surrey Doubles Tournament. We noticed nobody from our A Team had entered. Lulu had asthma all weekend so it was hit-the-ball-and-drag-Lulu the whole time. I'm getting too old for this.

Love, your flagging sister

10

Gunpowder, Treason, and Plot

The Isle of Wight off the south coast promotes itself as "Britain's Playground: Five miles wide and thirteen miles across, with 500 miles of footpaths." I had visions of an army of backpackers with their walking sticks, trudging slackjawed in criss-cross patterns over the countryside. Still, a vague lure by this maritime outpost prompted us one Saturday morning to drive down the Portsmouth Road again and take the fifteen-minute ferry ride across the Spithead to find the promised "Fall Getaway Weekend of Adventure."

IOW is one of those areas of Britain untouched by time. Everything remains exactly as it was originally built. Unfortunately, almost the entire place looks like it was thrown together about 1951, a year that surely sits in the nadir of the last millennium's architectural achievement. Post-war Britain was obsessed with utility and frugality. As we drove through the towns of IOW – Ryde, Nettlestone, Brading, Wooten Bridge – street after street of rowhouses looked like third prize in a kindergarten crayola contest – peaked roof, door, window, chimney; peaked roof, door, window, chimney ... Slate colored skies and steady drizzle didn't help our initial impressions: after almost 50 years of weathering, the Isle of Wight looked depressingly more like the Isle of Blight.

Undaunted and ever hopeful, we pressed on to the seaside resort of Sandown. We had read in *Greatest Golf Courses in the British Isles* that the Cliffsides

Hotel offered "pleasant accommodations, charming views of the sea, and access to fine golf. That seemed a good enough recommendation to book a room for the weekend.

In the shallow car park in front of Cliffsides, Eileen turned to me and suggested we check the publication date of *Best Golf Courses*. Cliffsides must have been a welcome sight to vacationers – in 1960. More crayola lines. Faded pastel panels hung tenuously on an otherwise bare façade. Air conditioning units sagged from the windows ("for your individual comfort control"). Dispiritingly drab brick buildings of indeterminate color abutted either side

I'm not the first person to notice the nostalgic connection between music and architecture. Whenever I hear Gregorian chant, for example, I conjure up visions of a cathedral in the Vatican with stone walls and marble pillars giving its unique echo chamber resonance. The thunderous "We will we will rock you" always makes me think of a cavernous arena, with 30,000 people cheering their local basketball team to gladiatorial victory. "On Britannia" reminds me of Big Ben atop Parliament and the Gothic spires of Westminster Abbey.

So what would I associate with Cliffsides? Have you ever heard a piano tuner work his way painfully through all eighty-eight keys, comparing each to his tuning forks? Bing-bing-bing. Bong. Adjust. Bing-bing-bing. Bong. Adjust. That's about it for Cliffsides.

We could see the misty English Channel through the windows at the back of the brown linoleumed lobby. Despite the tatiness of it all, I sensed the promise of a glass of Harvey's Bristol Cream sherry as we sat on a couch in our sea view room. Eileen wasn't as convinced. "This place looks like the beach at Coney Island at low tide."

The young girl behind the counter fumbled through a deck of index cards when we announced our arrival. She selected one and stared at it and then gave us the frightened doe look. "I'm sorry sir. All our water view rooms have been taken. A coachload of guests just cleared a few moments ago."

"But I have a reservation. It says you have reserved a room for us with a view of the water. You'll have to find us a sea view room." Eileen had folded her arms and set her jaw, in a position for full frontal assault.

The young girl continued, "I'm sorry, but all the rooms are spoken for. Perhaps one of our garden view rooms will do …"

My explosive protests roused from the back office a slow moving, pallid figure with a Duty Manager badge pinned to his chest. I had the feeling it was his job to give us a load of duty. "Uh, I'm Mr. Sembly-Mapleston. It seems, uh, we had an unusual flow of bookings arrive this morning, all for sea view. Quite impossible to move them now. Perhaps one of our garden rooms…?"

"But (you dolt, I wanted to add) the reason people vacation on an island is because it's surrounded by water. That's why we made a reservation for a sea view room. That's why we sent you a forty pound deposit. So it would be reserved for us. Why would I want a garden view?"

"Uh, I'm sorry sir…"

Despite my nearly uncontained wrath, we agreed to look at the garden view rooms. Down narrow, dim halls, up and down half staircases, we followed him. In one murky passageway we stopped as the door to a semi-private WC opened. An attractive lady stepped out and quickly closed the door. She must have thought I was the first in a queue of three. With apprehension in her eyes she said in a low voice, "You might give it a moment."

Through more corridors we plodded behind the Duty Manager until he said, "Uh, here it is." He flung open the door, which immediately crashed into the bed. He didn't make any move to lead us in.

We have been in disheartening hotel rooms before, but we kicked ourselves for not bringing along the Grand Prize Cup. No more than eight by ten with brown carpet, brown lampshade, brown bedcovers, tan walls. It was sort of early Newcastle Miner's Cottage decor. For a moment I fantasized about getting up tomorrow morning and trudging off to the coal pits in my hardhat, pick and shovel in hand.

Out the single window I saw our estate wagon sitting in the car park. I noticed the skeleton of a shrub just outside that must have been the garden. Neither Eileen nor I could muster the courage to check the bathroom.

"I don't think so," Eileen announced.

"Please give us our deposit back. We'll find something somewhere." I said to Mr. Sembly-Mapleston.

The Duty Manager gave us a disconsolate shrug, but then shifted his eyes from side to side in a conspiratorial gesture. "Uh, you might want to try *The Chestnuts*," he whispered. "It's about a half mile down the coast. They may suit your needs. Just walk down our road straight-away and turn left past the Shanklin Chine."

With £40 in hand, we walked down the coast road, I with my travel planning prowess besmirched, Eileen with an amused scowl. We passed a large sign announcing the Shanklin Chine, whose entrance price was £2. Neither of us knew what a chine was or why we'd want to part with £2 to see one. In another hundred meters we skirted around a white gate across a narrow lane. The transformation so stunned us that we had to turn around to see what happened. The rowhouses and dense-packed hotels had abruptly ended and given way to the dense foliage of mature trees. Elms, beeches, and birches abounded. We had caught them at the moment before undress. The beeches had turned golden yellow. The maples had a hint of red. The others covered a spectrum from yellow to purple hues. What a glorious time to wander into a woodland.

"You know what this reminds me of?" I asked Eileen. Since I knew she didn't, I continued. "Frank Capra's *Lost Horizons.* Ronald Coleman and his troupe were caught on a Nepal mountain during a freak snowstorm. They only survived when a local sherpa led them to a passageway in the mountain's side that magically delivered them to Shangri-La, the tropical paradise."

"Wonderful, sherpa," she said caustically. "Keep walking and let's see if you can find *us* a Shangri-La."

The Chestnuts lay at the back of an impossibly lush lawn with bordering flower gardens resplendent with color. Beyond, through the trees we could see the Channel. The mist had begun to lift and we could make out a few boats plodding towards unknown destinations. *The Chestnuts* looked more like a large summer home than a hotel. Its wattle and daub must have been recently painted. The brown, rough-hewn beams cut the fresh white plaster into bright sections. Small glass windows with diamond-shaped leaded panes checkered the two sides of the house we could see. An ancient chestnut tree stood guard along the front walk. Hundreds of green prickly spheres hung from the branches like tiny medieval flails. Even more lay in the grass. Those that fell on the flagstone walk had cracked and exposed soft brown chestnuts, some completely out of their barbed covers.

The Chestnut's front door looked capable of withstanding an attack of invading Frisians from across the Channel. Thick iron straps held together heavy oak timber. Knocking seemed useless, but Eileen spied a bell atop a black wrought iron fixture. The handle refused to respond to my tugs. In frustration I tried to loosen it by twisting the fixture's handle and heard the ring of an electric doorbell somewhere inside. Surprised but encouraged, I twisted it again and heard the same sound. "Good sign," I said to Eileen. "They've got electricity."

In seconds a girl of no more than ten appeared from behind the door, wide-eyed with long and limp dark hair that framed an expressionless face. No greeting came from her, just a stare. "We're looking for a sea view room for tonight," I said.

Our greeter turned and fled down the hall. "Do you suppose," I asked, "this might be the site of one of those Gothic English novels? You know, where nobody in the household talks except a wizened old proprietress. And she wears a severe black dress down to the floor, with ruffles at the neck and wrists. And at night we'll hear some one dragging chains upstairs and wind whistling down the hallway. And …"

"'Ello mate. Wot can Oi do for ya?"

A green and yellow Hawaiian print shirt hung straight down from his barrel chest. One arm had a tattoo of a rose garden, the other "MUM" in the center of a red heart pierced by a blue cross. White paint was spattered liberally over him. He clutched the self-incriminating brush in his hand.

"We were looking for a room for the night. With a view of the sea."

His face lit up as if I had a Publishers Clearinghouse check in my hand.

"Well, come in and I'll show you what we 'ave. Pardon me appearance. We're doing a little late season dress-up before we close up for the winter. This is my little girl, Amanda. Say 'ello, Amanda."

The saucer-eyed girl backed behind the Hawaiian shirt and continued to stare at us as if we had horns.

"Jack's my name. Are you Yanks? Well of course you are, with that accent. Just visiting, are you? Well, what else would you be doing, asking for a room for the night and all? Right?"

Jack rattled on in his thick East London accent with this continuous litany of questions and answers as he led us down the hall to a staircase. At the top we read a sign announcing, "FIRST FLOOR." As in all other British hotels, we had just come from the "GROUND FLOOR" and were now on the "FIRST FLOOR," not the "SECOND FLOOR," which was above us on the third floor.

A dark hall headed towards the back of the building. Jack flipped the light switch down (not up, in this country) and then toggled it a few times. "Must have just burned out. Isn't that always the way? Always the way."

Eileen frantically brushed something away from her face. "Those spider webs. They pop up on a moment's notice, don't they? They do. Don't you just hate that? I do."

This man could carry on a conversation with a mime. "'Ere it is, best room in the place. Isn't that a view? Beautiful, if you ask me."

To our surprise we had entered a large, cheery room with imposing French doors opening to a balcony that faced a great expanse of the Channel through a gap in the cliffside woods. A few sailboats close in and commercial craft further out completed the land- and seascape.

"It ain't heaven, but it's quite pleasant. Thirty-nine quid the night. Includes a proper breakfast. Do you want to stay? I guess you do. I'll be downstairs if you want to change your mind."

"First time you ever made a deal without having to say a word," Eileen said to me after he left. My shrewd competence in finding this place had improved her mood and restored my image.

On our way out a little later to see the local sights, we asked Jack to recommend a place for dinner. "Hang on. Won't you want to go to Guy Fawkes Night first? Well of course you will. You can come with me and Amanda and the wife. But finding a table in a restaurant after that will be like looking for rocking horse shit in the Queen's paddock. Pardon me language ma'am. But I know the publican at the Slug and the Lettuce in Bembridge and he'll get you fed."

"Guy Fawkes Night?"

With only the slightest bit of encouragement, Jack launched into the history and tradition of Guy Fawkes.

"Remember, remember, the fifth of November
Gunpowder, treason, and plot.
Remember the reason
For gunpowder treason
Shall not be forgot.

"That's the rhyme that goes with it. You see Guy Fawkes had this plot about three hundred years ago to destroy Parliament by blowing it up while they was in session. Somehow he was discovered before the dirty deed could be committed. So what'd they do to him? He was drawn and quartered and all. Now Guy Fawkes Night is celebrated on the anniversary by a bonfire and fireworks. How long they been doing this? As long as I can remember."

I thought I'd break into the conversation. "What exactly are people celebrating, Jack?"

"Well, that's it. We don't exactly know. That's because you can read the rhyme either way. A warning to the Government or to the plotters. Anyway, we've got no bank holidays between summer and Christmas, so don't we need something to take our minds off working? We do, we do."

Jack promised to take us to the celebration if we returned by early evening. "I take Amanda and the wife every year. So why don't you join us? No reason. See you at six for a little fortification before we go."

******

The crown jewel of the IOW sits on the north side, on a knoll overlooking the Solent, the channel between the small and the big islands. There, Victoria and Albert built a retreat from Buckingham while she was Queen. With our golf washed out by torrential rain, we decided to salvage the afternoon by taking a tour of the huge Osbourne House, another frozen-in-time accommodation, this one being from the late nineteenth century.

"Four pounds seventy," demanded a taut-lipped woman at the door, dressed in an old Aeroflot flight attendant's uniform, or close to it. Behind her stood a gent in livery from another era. If V & A were still in residence, he would have no doubt been their manservant. Hands folded on his waistcoated stomach, he pursed his lips and sucked in his cheeks as if he had canker sores that needed licking. His head tilted back and he eyeballed us through imaginary bifocals. The two of them made us feel like we had stepped in something on the way in or had just split an infinitive. Actually, Jeeves cracked a smile and "rah-ther" when Eileen said something about there being enough rain to float the IOW back up the River Bourne.

As we wandered through Osbourne House, we came across enough opulence to remind us how the British mesmerize themselves with the conspicuous consumption of the aristocratic class and tolerate the huge gaps between the entitled and the disenfranchised. Americans do it sometimes, but few of the iceberg-tip rich, the really rich, put their wealth on such display. But the English do and they love it, apparently content to ever be the have-nots. Gold leaf ceilings, grand halls, sculptured gardens, Osbourne House had all the trappings.

As the story goes, the Prince Consort, Albert, died a premature death from overwork when he and Victoria were in their thirties. The two of them had cut dashing figures, based on the dazzling, life-sized portraits strewn among the dozen reception rooms. In her grief after he died, Victoria either became a raging chocoholic or developed some other untoward eating disorder. By the end of her life she had achieved Guinness Record Book status. Her girth allegedly equaled her height. She was one big lady.

The brochure told us that down by the waterside we could see her "bathing machine." In the latter part of the nineteenth century, swimming became regarded as a healthy pastime. To protect her modesty, Victoria had a wooden bathhouse on wheels built to transport her right into the water, where she could slosh around unobserved by the unwashed masses. I suspected that in addition to her obsessive eating she had a Moby Dick complex. The vision of Her Royal Cetacean thrashing about in a wooden crate dampened our enthusiasm for the walk down to the site, even more than the incessant rain.

"In her declining years she had an elevator installed," a docent told us. "Unfortunately, the house was not yet wired for electricity. Several men in the cellar worked a hand crank to draw her to the first floor. Poor devils," she sniffed.

"The highlight of Osbourne House sits here in the Royal Bedroom, "another Aeroflot stew told us." On the Royal Bed you see a little cloth sack that held Albert's pocket watch. A small, depressing, posthumous painting of Albert still lies on the pillow." She didn't say depressing, but it was. "Victoria lived 40 years longer than Albert, but every night she took him to bed with her." Yeah, that and a box of bonbons. Some role model for the country.

Across the room sat the Royal Chaise Lounge on which the Queen passed away in 1901. Being American I wanted to ask, "You mean that large lady lay on that little couch and the sucker didn't collapse?" But I refrained. We had already paid for the night's lodgings on the island.

******

"Be a little damp, what with the rain," Jack said to us at *The Chestnuts* as we left for the Guy Fawkes celebration. He handed us each a green vinyl trash bag. "Here, take these bin liners with you in case it gets bad. You know what to do with them, right? Punch some holes in the bottom and pull them over your head."

He stuffed us in his two door Peugeot, along with the wife, his dog, Riffle, and little, wide-eyed Amanda. Jack had volunteered the dog's name, but not the wife's. "Shelly," we found out by asking her ourselves.

In a few minutes, we came to a broad, miry field where carneys had set up their rides and booths – ring tosses, a cotton candy stand (at which I treated Amanda), a kiddy Ferris wheel, and cars that snap you around in circles till you throw up the cotton candy. My favorite to watch was *The Crank*. Fifteen people sat strapped to a bench facing the crowd. Spotlights came on, canned music started, and the crank moved the bench like a bicycle pedal, up and around and down, then in the opposite direction. The fifteen sat with embarrassed looks as if they should be enjoying themselves but didn't quite know why. After about five minutes of this to'ing and fro'ing, they got off, and another fifteen from the queue took their places. It was a sight that one does not easily forget.

"Should we look for a place to watch the bonfire?" asked Jack. "We better."

We slogged through the mud to a crowd gathering at the fence of the adjacent heath, waiting for something to happen. The night had settled into another of those Cornwall mists. People began donning their bin liners and we followed suit. In few minutes, we looked like an army of vinyl mushrooms, with heads and arms poking out the tops and green gum boots out the bottoms.

At seven-thirty flames began to lick at the bottom of a huge pyramid of debris. Applause and cheers arose from the crowd of five hundred. In about seven minutes, a huge blaze enveloped the entire forty-foot high pile.

Big fires fascinate most people. They exude a sense of primal force – at least for a while. But after watching a bonfire burn for about fifteen minutes, everyone slowly comes to the realization that this pile of trash might burn all night, and they have to stand there in endless impatience watching it because that's what everyone else is doing. Luckily, after several centuries of this, somebody had figured out that if they used old wooden pallets for the firewood, the bonfire would burn with an uncommon sense of urgency, what with pallets being mostly airspace. After forty minutes the entire inferno had settled into a pile of glowing embers. Even that was more than enough for me and I squished the mud with my feet in cadence with the rest of the crowd until an extraordinary display of fireworks announced itself by two starbursts detonated directly above our heads.

British fireworks are more intimate than the American equivalent. For the next half-hour we watched and heard continuous, I mean non-stop, displays of rockets, pinwheels, fountains, sprays, and detonations. Most of them were set off at about fifteen feet above ground level, maybe 30 meters away. They gave the impression we could easily reach out and have our fingertips blown away. Every few minutes I'd think, "Well, this must be the finale," as they saturated the field with color and noise. But on they would go in a rush of booming light. Like the effect of pyrotechnics everywhere, we came away dazzled by the sight, sound, and resonance.

"Who sponsors such a thing?" we asked Jack on the way back to *The Chestnuts*. "Who pays for it all?"

"You took the question right out of me mouth. It's a charity thing. The two quid we pays at the gate goes to charity and the local shopkeepers pay for the fireworks. Happens all over Britain on Guy Fawkes Night. Ain't that a nice thing? It certainly is."

The next morning Jack fed us his proper breakfast – eggs, mushrooms, tomatoes, bacon, bangers, blood pudding, beans, fried toast, and coffee and insisted we finish it all. Then he sent us off in our car to see a real chine. "You don't want to see that little scratch in

Shanklin that they charges you two quid for, do you? No, of course not. Go out to the south coast and see the real chines."

The Isle of Wight is composed mostly of chalk and clay. As time passes, rainwater run-off slowly washes the clay away from the chalk. The island is a favorite hunting ground for paleontologists and stratigraphers who get it off by looking for petrified troglodytes and bug droppings. At one of the overlooks along the windblown cliffs, we saw a dozen or so people poking and scratching a nearby clay outcrop with sticks and spoons. While I parked the car, Eileen went up and found them to be on a field trip from the local community college. I guessed something like that before I caught up, but I couldn't resist an opportunity. When I reached the professor obviously in charge, I asked him in as loud a voice as was polite, "Did you lose a contact lens or something? Can I help look?"

I got a few titters, but mostly blank stares. He went on to enthusiastically show Eileen the snails and clamshells they had plucked from the mucky clay, two hundred feet above sea level. Avoiding the appearance of wholly ignoring me, he asked one of the students to help me with directions to the Blackgang Chine and the Whale Chine, another mile down the road.

We almost missed the obscure historic marker at the rough car park next to the Whale Chine. It described a chine as a ravine cut through the cliff at a point where rain runoff finds an accumulation of erodible clay. Scientists had concluded that Whale Chine had taken about 17,000 years to achieve its present condition. This particular chine had been used for decades as access to a Lifeboaters' station. As best

I can figure, the Lifeboaters are an obscure cult of maritime Samaritans. I had seen donation boxes at pubs for them. They wait around in isolated villages near the coast for ships to founder, then run to their lifeboats, drag them to the water, and rescue survivors. The historical marker indicated that the Whale Chine had recently gotten too steep for the Lifeboaters and they no longer pulled their crafts up and down the rugged cleft. It didn't say whether shipwreck victims were now hopelessly on their own or if help was still at hand.

We heard the gurgle of water coming from a tangle of brambles next to the car park. Along a path towards the sea, a rivulet of water emerged from the undergrowth in a small gash in the ground. In the next hundred yards it enlarged to a dramatically huge fissure. At the cliff's edge, the chine measured maybe a hundred feet across and two hundred feet down to the beach. Water from yesterday's rain cascaded in an undirected route down the crevasse.

Some civic-minded organization had built a crude stairway down the chine, as steep a set of steps as we had ever navigated. We carefully made our way down to the shallow beach. Looking back up, the edges of the chine were so sharp the cliff appeared to have impetuously ruptured from strain rather than erosion.

We returned to the car and pushed on, anxious to see the mysterious sounding Blackgang Chine, another half mile down the road. It was our fortune to have already climbed the Whale Chine. Some indecorous entrepreneur had erected the Blackgang Chine Amusement Park at this clifftop, complete with a forty-foot fiberglass pirate, blinking road signs, tacky amusement center, and a two-acre car park. We fled.

We returned to *The Chestnuts* and collected our belongings. Jack, Amanda, and the wife bid us goodbye as we made prevaricated promises about quick returns.

"Won't we look forward to that Amanda? We will, we will."

On our way back through the grim mid-century architecture of Bradley, Nettlestone, Wooten Bridge and Ryde, we concluded that the chines probably change as fast as anything else does on IOW.

November 2

Dear Richard,

Judy, Sue, and Sandra came to visit for a few days and had trouble adjusting to British utilities. Sandra plugged her electric toothbrush into an adapter we use for lamps, thinking it was a transformer. She came back a little while later to find a pile of molten plastic on the dresser. Judy tried her hair curler with the adapter she brought from America and Sue noticed her hair starting to smolder. Now she's got a bald spot on top. Sue got into our new but tiny power shower stall okay but couldn't figure how to get the folding glass doors open from the inside. She finally yelled for help and Bill had to talk her through it from outside the bathroom door.

I took them down to Arundel in West Sussex and showed them a real castle. Notched walls, towers, turrets, and all. The Dukes of Norfolk have owned Arundel Castle since the sixteenth century, and while we were touring, we bumped into an affable little man showing some friends around the grounds. It was the present Duke himself, all friendly and talkative. "I love Americans," he explained. "Saved us from those bloody Nazis. Thank goodness for Pearl Harbor." We expressed some shock at that. "If it weren't for that," he explained," You Yanks would never have entered the war and we'd have been lost. Sorry about all your casualties and that, but it did save our country from invasion."

TJDGI #9: When we first got here, Bill had gone to a specialty shop on The Strand in London that sold coffee and tea. He asked where the flavored de-caf coffee was and the clerk said they didn't carry it, just flavored <u>with</u> caffeine. "All this variety of coffee and you don't have flavored de-caf. When do you suppose people drink de-caf?" He thought perhaps mostly at night. "And when would people drink flavored coffee?" Also almost always at night, he suggested. "Then how come you don't carry flavored de-caf?" He thought for a moment. "Hang on. You might have something there." Bill was there again last week. Still no flavored decaf.

Halloween is a minor holiday here, but in celebration we put three pumpkins on our front steps. To no surprise, the first morning after, we found one missing and later saw it smashed on the road to the train station. Second morning, the second one was gone. Almost time for Constable Woosely to add an entry to our case number. The third day, about 4:30, I heard a timid knock at the front door and found an eight year old moppet standing there in a shabby coat about two sizes too big. "Could I have your pumpkin, Mum?" I was so surprised I asked him why he wanted it. "For Halloween, Mum." Of course I gave him the pumpkin and even a Mars Bar. And thanked him for asking.

Love, your softhearted sister

11

Pheasants

Jack and I both agreed. We deserved a day in the heath on a proper pheasant hunt, even if it cost as much as the whole waterfowl season in Texas. His company, like mine, had transplanted him to Britain and the two of us had to give up our perennial duck hunting lease on the prairie west of Houston.

Jack had made a few discreet inquiries at the local sporting goods shop in his town, Winchester. "I think I might be able to line up something with the locals," he told me in October. Sure enough in November, he called back and said, "I've got it. The first Saturday in December. And that's the week our wives are off to the German Christmas market. Perfect." Then he lowered his voice a few tones. "It's a little expensive. Three hundred pounds for the day …"

"No problem," I said, as enthusiastically as I could manage. "That's about as much as we've saved by not duck hunting. Right?"

"Right. Right." Like two old drunks supporting each other on bar stools, we continued to rationalize how we quite rightly deserved to treat ourselves once in a while.

We gathered from our instructions that a proper pheasant shoot was more civilized than what we waterfowlers were used to. Activities would begin at the decent time of 8:30 a.m., not four hours earlier. Of course that turned out to be little advantage since December dawns don't arrive until eight anyway. We should expect refreshments at mid-morning and lunch at half-noon. Attire should be appropriate. We thought a phone call about "appropriate" might be in order, lest we unwittingly embarrass our nation and ourselves.

Saturday morning we met at Jack's front door in our agreed-upon, suitable attire. Neither of us could bring ourselves to invest in proper tweed plus-fours. And certainly jeans or khakis wouldn't do. So we donned our oldest wool trousers and stuffed the pant legs into some nubby woolen socks.

"Neckwear is not obligatory. Some choose not to wear it, "Jack had heard our guide sniff. "Americans, mostly."

We wore our drabbest brown ties over tatersall shirts, especially purchased for the occasion. Below our threepenny caps we wore our green L. L. Bean coats. "Do you think these will pass for the wax jackets we saw in the sport shop?" I asked Jack.

"Not unless we rip out all the Goretex© and then pour hot paraffin all over the outside to get the smell right."

We stamped our wellies in the misty dawn to keep warm, but in just a few minutes the raw dampness of the Winchester heath started to creep through our layered insulation. This was the kind of morning that was better for shooting some gloomy movie like the *Hounds of Baskerville* than for shooting birds.

Our guide arrived to lead us to the countryside and Jack introduced him as Roger Bagger. I stifled a guffaw. How many in this country, I asked myself, let their names lead them to their occupations. I knew

Roger Rainbow, the chap in my office that did our long range planning. Oliver Sparrow was our roving intelligence scout, and Timothy Precious, our records keeper. Now comes Roger Bagger to take us on a hunt.

We followed Roger in Jack's Volvo Saloon to the farm of the shootmaster. As we rolled into the parking area, we heard a sniggering voice accompanying elbows in the ribs among the three or four shooters already there. "Know the difference between a porcupine and a Volvo Saloon?"

"What's that?"

"A porcupine has pricks are on the outside."

Chortles and snorts followed as Jack and I traded uneasy looks. "Sounds like our arrival had advance notice," I said.

Within a few minutes, the shootmaster called us all to assembly in the forecourt. Duncan Moresly introduced himself to the group of eight. "Let me rehearse for you the general rules of the shoot. We will place you at each stand where you will stay until the shoot at that venue is complete. No wandering. No shooting at ground game. No squirrels. No rabbits. Shoot at a pheasant only if you see sky behind him. The beaters will appreciate that. Give them a good lead and shoot them in the head. The butcher has a hard time selling them if they are mutilated with a full body shot. No shooting at white pheasants. Twenty-five quid fine for anyone who takes one down."

At the mention of white pheasants, Jack and I looked at each other with eyebrow shrugs. I raised my hand and asked Duncan, "Could you tell me what a white pheasant is?"

Duncan's face sagged. His eyes rolled back. "It's going to be that kind of day, is it?" he groaned. "You're the Americans, eh? A white pheasant is a pheasant that's white. Whiter than that mourning dove on the fence rail there. Albino. We just don't shoot them. We send the twenty-five quid to local charity to make the point."

Then he lowered his head, squinted, and asked about our shooting experience. Jack and I assured him that we had hunted together for at least twelve seasons and done plenty of shooting. This was, however, our first English shoot, and Jack's first pheasant hunt. Duncan seemed underwhelmed with our credentials.

Despite his skepticism, he loaded six of us into the back of his lorry. Two more followed in a special rig. Gilbert was nearly paralyzed below the waist, but he was still an avid gamesman. His young companion, David, drove him and towed a trailer with a four-wheel All Terrain Vehicle.

Duncan carried us about three miles to the first meadow and copse, a most agreeable place to shoot pheasants. He opened a leather case of eight plastic collar stay-looking things. I watched closely as the other shooters performed a ritual selection, and when offered, picked one myself. It was indeed shaped like a stay, but mine had the number one printed on it. Jack was two.

Duncan announced the first rotation. "Number one at the point; two in the meadow; three at the wall ..." I took up my position at the point of the copse. Jack moved about 60 paces into the field. We broke open our double-barreled shotguns and waited with anticipation. Slowly I became aware of a person standing behind me, and I also noticed Duncan standing not far behind Jack.

"Mornin' sir. I'm Godfrey. 'Ave any questions, just ask me." Apparently we had not yet impressed Duncan with our American field skills and he'd rather not have us shoot each other or ourselves. Godfrey continued. "When you 'ear the beater getting close, you just watch that point and you'll see the tiddlers start to fly."

In about five minutes we began to hear yelps, whistles, grunts, and banging from an untold number of people moving through the woods towards us. "Ready now," murmured Godfrey. "There."

A huge cock pheasant burst from the woods to my right with a piercing cackle and clamorous wingbeat. I put my gun up, led him about eight feet, and fired once. The bird folded and fell, landing five paces from me. A second cock came out to the left before I could reload, but I used my remaining round and downed him. A third flew off to the center of the meadow. Jack took him down with one shot.

In about ten minutes, I had fired six times at four pheasants and gotten them all; Jack had taken three of the four that went his way. When we tallied the results back at the lorry, the eight of us had taken twelve pheasants. With little ado, we unloaded guns and loaded ourselves into the lorry. As we pulled away, a half dozen dogs and handlers emerged soundlessly from the morning mist and begin to scour the fields for our take. We drove off to the next stand.

"Number two on the knoll; three near the oak; four at the brook..." Neither Duncan followed Jack, nor did Godfrey shadow me at this stand. Apparently we had demonstrated our field acumen. Godfrey could resume his duties as beater and Duncan as impresario. Timing is everything because Jack's and my shooting deteriorated at this stand, with each of us taking only two from six shots.

Gilbert, our invalid companion in his sixties, kept up without fail. At each stand, his friend David would back the ATV off the trailer. Gilbert would don his two aluminum crutches and work his way into to the saddle. Crossing the six-foot distance was painful to watch but the whole way he wore a grin that said, "I'm just happy to be here." Off he would motor to his appointed stand, where he would pull his shotgun out of its scabbard and a handful of shells out of his saddle bags. Like John Wayne reincarnated, he shot right from the saddle.

About 10:30, between shoots, Duncan opened a hidden compartment in the back of the lorry. "Refreshments gentlemen. You can help yourselves to the Stilton cheese and leeks on crackers, the sliced Cumberland sausage, and so on. To complement that, I offer you a Pimm's Cup or, if you'd rather, ginger wine and cognac."

I opted for the ginger wine concoction, just the antidote for the chilly mist that still followed us that day. I drank only half a glassful before the humidity dropped noticeably. Jack opted for the Pimm's and then he nudged me. "Get that. Everything looks so la-dee-da until you notice that at the back of the tray." He pointed discreetly at an improbable red canister with the inscription,

PRINGLES.
BARBECUE FLAVOR

When everyone else heartily accepted a second round of drinks, Jack and I glanced at each other. To us card-carrying Ducks Unlimited members, mixing alcohol and gunpowder was verboten. But I restrained my comments, thinking that we Texans might not be the best judges of how one should behave in an advanced civilization.

More shoots. More pheasants. At midday we stopped for mugs of hot tomato soup, the rest of the Pringles, and prawn mayonnaise sandwiches, which surprised me by not tasting like someone left an open jar of Hellman's mayo in the sun for a week.

Somewhere in the middle of the afternoon shoots, Duncan asked Jack and me, "You are going to join us for dinner after the shoot?"

Jack and I spontaneously agreed to this unanticipated opportunity. Duncan leaned over to us and said in a worried sotto *voce*, "We're, uh, having a roast of pork. You don't have any, uh, thing about that, do you?"

"No problem," we assured him, a bit puzzled.

As Duncan left to resume his role as maestro, I said to Jack, "We must look either Jewish, Muslim, or like former trichinosis victims."

By 3:00 we arrived at our last stand, and spread ourselves along a steep hill below a growth of ancient oak and hickory. Jack stood to my left. To my right Gilbert sat on his four-wheeler, which tilted perilously on the slope. The overcast sky atop the trees was already turning to dusk and the cold dampness further penetrated to our tired bones. Still, as the sounds of the beaters drove the cackling birds to us, the adrenaline began to pump once more. Again cocks flew to the left and right and we took them as best we could. What was to be the last bird of the day burst out of the trees flew directly toward me. I snapped my gun to my shoulder and fired. Despite a burst of feathers, the big bird veered to my right. The thought crossed my mind, "That bird's dead and he doesn't know it."

In tandem, my face paled and Gilbert's eyes widened in alarm as we both watched the bird fold its wings and swoon into Gilbert's chest with a resonating thump. Off went Gilbert and over went the ATV, fortunately in another direction. The other shooters stared for a few seconds, uncertain whether to gasp or laugh. At once the woods erupted with people of all ages, scrambling to Gilbert's assistance. In a flash they had him again back in the saddle, upright and unhurt. They surrounded him with sounds of concern, a din in which the only recognizable and recurrent words were, "so sorry…"

My concern with Gilbert's safe recovery gave way to confusion. Who were these people? Descendants of Robin Hood's band of merry men? A lost company of itinerant leprechauns? Slowly it came to me. For the first time I had more than a glimpse of the beaters, a crew of all types and sizes. I saw a lad no more than eight; a gentlemen near eighty; men, ladies and teenagers, all local town folk, rending the same services their ancestors had for centuries, and doing it with the same personal concern for safety of the shooters. Almost all were dressed in common fashion, a sort of countryman's camouflage – wellies, heavy loden trousers, dark green waxed midcoats and caps.

Back at the farm after a full day, we tallied the results. One hundred and eight pheasants … and not one white. Jack had twelve, I had sixteen. Ignoring any possible rules of decorum, we made our shooting companions pose for photos with us.

"Here," Duncan offered. "Each of you hold your brace in one hand and your gun in the other." He handed us a leather strap with a pheasant hung on each end.

******

Neither Jack nor I were quite prepared for the promised supper, a fine table set in the large dining room-kitchen of Duncan's simple farmhouse. Duncan briefly introduced his wife and daughter as they labored over steaming pots and the oven. He offered drinks to all and I was careful to ask for "whiskey," not "scotch."

Duncan handed me a glass. "Lagavulin, finest of the single malts."

The small tumbler had no more than a third of an inch of whiskey in it, and Duncan seemed totally nonplussed about it. He poured the same diminutive amount for another shooter and my paranoia dissipated.

Being now a connoisseur of single malt whiskeys, I tipped my glass to Duncan and then took the most meager of sips in order not to drain it. Once again as I swallowed, vapors from the dark brown fluid filled my nasal passages with the bouquet of smoky peat – even though peat is not a smell that one normally associates with the word bouquet. Whether it was the fatiguingly long day of stamping around in the cold damp or the Scottish distiller's scrupulous aging, the whiskey tasted wonderfully hardy. It was quite unlike the Cutty Sark or J&B or even the Old Fettercairn I had been thinking about when I had said, "Whiskey please."

The nine of us sat down to an imposing five-course meal centered on a roasted piglet. (Praise be either to Allah, Yahweh, or my Internist, we could eat it.) Commodious servings of wine elicited relaxed conversation, riveting hunting tales, and other explications of testosterone in the pursuit of blood sport. Despite the mountainous bounty and second helpings served silently by mother and daughter, Duncan admonished us to save room for dessert. His wife, her hands buried in a large towel, removed a steaming dish from the oven behind me.

My salivary glands dried up abruptly when the dish reached my end of the table. As inexplicable as the barbecue Pringles, I held in my hand an aluminum foil pan of Sara Lee Cinnamon Coffeecake. Ah well …

After the Sara Lee disappeared, Duncan brought in a cut crystal decanter and announced, "Gentlemen. Port," and began the bottle around the table. At my turn, I poured a dram into my own sculptured crystal port glass and moved the bottle to Gilbert on my left. By the time it got around the table and past Jack, it was empty. Duncan, ever the gracious host, immediately retrieved another bottle and said, "Gentlemen, this time even better. Cockburn seventy-eight," which came out as "Coe-burn seventy-ite."

A reverent quiet fell over the table. Duncan tenderly opened the bottle. His wife brought him a sparkling fresh decanter and he slowly and gently poured the port into it. I waited for the table conversation resumed to cover my ignorance and asked Gilbert what was going on. "That bottle has likely been standing on his shelf for five years," he told me under his cupped hand. "The crusty sediment has sunk to the bottom. That's why he is decanting it ever so carefully."

That's why we call them decanters, I said to myself.

With the pride and pomp of a Savoy sommelier, Duncan passed the refilled decanter to Robert, the next in line and across the table from me. Hearing the murmurs of anticipation, and having already finished my own port, I said to Robert, "He makes it sound very special. I'd like to have a taste." As I extended my glass across the table, Robert put the palm of his free hand to his chest and looked aghast. Now what had I done?

"Well I ... I can't," he stammered.

All conversation had stopped. "Why is that?" I said, choosing my only honorable course, the dumb American.

"Well. It's protocol. You must pour it yourself. We pass the port to our left and each man must pour his own."

"Ah!" I said. "A wonderful custom. I guess I just have to be patient."

Robert's brow slowly relaxed and the corners of his eyes softened slightly. "Well, perhaps we might make an exception," he said, turning his head to the host for approval.

The table bubbled with "Yes, yes's," and "roight's," as Robert poured me a dram of Cockburn '78.

The evening wound down in mellow but unmemorable conversation. Duncan joined Jack and me as we left and put his arms over both our shoulders while we walked to the outbuilding where fifty-four braces of pheasants hung. "Not often we get Americans here, and they're hardly ever like you. It's been a pleasure shooting with such sportsman and even more, dining with such fine company. Would you do me the honor of taking home two braces tonight, not one?"

Sensing the honor, Jack and I were as effusive in our responses as our manliness would allow, offset in large part by our blood-alcohol content. In a hale of faire-thee-wells we sped off in our porcupine-mobile to Jack's house to pluck and clean our eight pheasants and enjoy a night of mindless sleep.

November 26

Dear Richard,

I've taken to walking into town instead of driving. The village is at least 400 years old and back then the sillies didn't think to leave much room on either side of the High Street for parking. I keep seeing old people walking by our house, rocking back and forth on their bad feet, pulling their trolleys to town. Every day an old man gets off his bicycle in front and walks it on, since that's as far up our hill he can pump. Luckily they all get to go downhill on the way home with their bundles. For a while I thought this town was full of just old people, but maybe they're out walking everywhere because they can't afford a car or just never did drive. Or I might be missing the whole point because they do it for the exercise.

The club championship is coming up in a month. Everyone on the D Team has signed up and we're waiting to see which of the A Team dares.

TJDGI #10: Bill bought a replacement bulb for our car headlight from the BP station in town, checking to ensure that he could return it if it was the wrong size. We went there Sunday to do that and the clerk said we'd have to come back the next day because BP doesn't do refunds on Sundays.

Scone alert. My buddy Ginger called me last night and told me that our supermarket has started to stock fresh scones. I expected to look out the window and see the searchlight with a scone on it emblazoned in the sky. I bought all eight off the shelf this morning.

We've invited the neighbors in the Close to a Christmas gift swap party, the kind we used to have

167

back home. I tried to explain that it's a game. After someone picks a gift out of the pile, they can have it "swapped" from them on the next person's turn. Then they'll have to pick again or steal someone else's. They've all been on the phone to each other in a twit, hoping that no one gets offended or unruly when they become a "swap victim."

I didn't tell you about the races. We all went to Sandown Racetrack across the street. The Queen Mum was there to run her horse and present the Whitbread Gold Cup. The old gal arrived in her Bentley, giving the Royal wave out the window – elbow bent, fingers up, rotation at the wrist. There's a picture there of her making the same award in 1939 when she was 38 years old. Her own horse lost this time so she didn't have to present the cup to herself. Later, when we adjourned to the Prince Albert Pub to end the day, we saw a picture of Herself taken there a few years back, behind the bar drawing a cool one from the tap. Lord, they love that old lady here.

Love, your mawkish sister

12

Ill Wind

It started atop the 6,286-foot peak of Jaggevane at the northern end of Norway's mountainous backbone. Heavy, cold air settled into the surrounding valleys, pushing the warmer air south. Like water in tributaries, air masses accumulated and plunged southward past the fjords and swept across the sea. Ninety-foot waves buffeted the offshore drilling platforms perched above the giant North Sea oil fields. By the time the winds reached the British Isles, they had sucked a trillion therms of energy from the Gulf Stream as it swung around the northern coast of Britain and then plunged to the North Sea's bottom, disappearing. Then fifty-mile winds pounded Aberdeen, Dundee, and Edinburgh, dropping ten inches of snow in their western suburbs.

The winds blew down the Midlands, past London, and howled across Sandown Golf Course. The flag poles on the greens bent like bows in the hands of powerful archers. At the south end of Sandown, this magnificent journey ended as winds slammed into Michael Court. The cold poured into our home through every conceivable orifice – around the window frames, under the front door, down the attic trap door, through the mail slot, the clothes drier vent, and through the mouse holes.

Window shades rippled and candles on the dining room table flickered to distraction. The boiler switched on at 5:45 in the morning and labored without interruption until it switched off at midnight. The house temperature never climbed above 17° C. We wore wool sweaters and flannel-lined pants as we hauled in cords of wood and scuttles of coal that disappeared in smoke up the chimney from a perpetual blaze in the fireplace.

"Doesn't seem to me quite as cold as you make it out to be," shouted Alistair, above the wind during a brisk walk to the pub on Sunday afternoon.

"Of course not," I said. "Since we live at the northern end of the close, we pre-heat the air for all of you. It comes in around the frame of our front door, we warm it up, and then it blows out our back door to all your houses.

"Well I must say that's bloody nice of you."

For about five days I nearly froze the ends of my most important appendages before my morning shower. I had taped plastic sheeting around the bathroom window in an attempt to simulate double-glazing. It bulged ominously into the room, like a distended bladder. I feared instantaneous frostbite the moment it burst.

"Maybe we should buy a space heater for the bathroom," Eileen suggested.

The village of Esher had its own electrical supply shop, a tiny one-story attached building no larger than the average bedroom. It had one of everything on its compact shelves. Jeremy Bentham proudly displayed his name on the hazy glass door, along with a six-digit telephone number. Esher Electrical is so old that the number predates the ten digit telephone numbers in use for the last four decades.

As Eileen and I walked in Saturday morning, Mr. Bentham, who predates contemporary commerce in the same way as his telephone number, was waiting on a customer. Their dialogue recaptured a time when a nation of shopkeepers catered to a simpler community.

"And are these fuses the only thing you need today, Mrs. Blemings?"

"Well, I do fancy those candle-shaped light bulbs there."

"Quite nice, aren't they?"

"Rather."

"Makes such lovely effect."

"Yes lovely. Do you have them in both threaded and bayonet base as well?"

"Oh, dear. I'm afraid I have them just in threaded. Sorry."

"Well, I'll just take four then."

"Lovely. Shall I wrap them for you?"

"That would be lovely."

Mr. Bentham selected four light bulbs and wrapped each carefully in brown paper and bagged them. "Oh, Mrs. Blemings, did you want me to test them?"

"Oh, that would be lovely."

I caught Eileen's eyes just before they rolled back into her head with a silent sigh. Then we watched Mr. Bentham demonstrate that each bulb would indeed light when connected to a power source, then re-wrap and bag them.

"Lovely, will there be anything else?"

At the moment of truth, Eileen and I held our breath. "Well I do need vacuum cleaner bags, but I'll get them another day."

I wondered if Mr. Bentham tested the vacuum cleaner bags as well.

"Six pounds sixty-two, including VAT for the Prime Minister."

"Yes, lovely," said Mrs. Blemings as she dug out the correct coins from her purse.

"Lovely," answered Mr. Bentham, sweeping up the cash. "Do mind the ice along the verge. It's quite treacherous today."

"Indeed, Mr. Bentham," she answered, tottling out the door, clutching the bag of candle-shape light bulbs.

"May I help you?"

With the exhilaration of a miler breaking the finish line tape, Eileen stepped forward. "Do you have any small, electric space heaters?"

No sooner were the words out of her mouth then the phone rang. Eileen's shoulders slumped as if she had just been disqualified for steroids and had her medal taken away.

Mr. Bentham never flinched. He carried on like a stone-deaf lip reader. "What size room?"

Ring-ring. Ring-ring.

"A bathroom, about six-by-six."

"A bathroom? Oh no, we can't sell space heaters for bathrooms."

Ring-ring. Ring-ring.

"You don't sell heaters for bathrooms? Why not?"

Ring-ring.

"Against the code. It's rather unsafe, with all the water, you know. You won't even find an outlet in your WC to plug it in."

I tried to recall an outlet in the bathroom, but couldn't

Ring-ring. Ring-ring

A product of his generation, Mr. Bentham had the civilized habit of dealing with his customers in the order in which they presented themselves, including those by telephone. Mr. Bentham gave no sign that he was going to answer the telephone until he had completed servicing us. We Americans couldn't stand a ringing telephone. Our culture demands that it be answered. Immediately. I have a friend whose daughter actually put a kidnapper on hold during a ransom call because she got a call-waiting signal. ("How much did you say – oh, could you hold for a minute? I've got another call coming in.")

"Why don't you go ahead and get that phone?"

"Oh, they'll wait or know enough to call back. It's no worry."

"Well then, do you have an electrical heater for, say, a six-by-six dressing room?"

Mr. Bentham stroked his chin with his thumb and forefinger, as if he was contemplating the possibility of chicanery. "Yes, yes, a dressing room. Perhaps we could find something.

He pulled a box from under the counter. "Could this be what you need? Two thousand watts, 21 hertz. If you need a five thousand, I can have it for you Tuesday."

Suspecting that Mr. Bentham would have the Royal Bathroom Police waiting for us Tuesday, we

175

agreed to purchase the smaller, but immediately available model. "If he offers to test it," Eileen whispered to me, "say no. Let's just pay and beat it."

As we completed our transaction, we traded three or four "lovelies" with Mr. Bentham He even slipped in a "brilliant" when I opted to pay by credit card, and an extra "lovely" when I signed the stub.

"Thanks ever so much for your custom," we heard as we left, minding the ice on the verge. We sneaked our illicit goods home.

Sure enough, our inspection yielded no outlet in the bathroom to plug in the heater. British building codes reflect their total paranoia about electricity, even though a portrait of Michael Faraday, the father of modern electricity, appears on the five-pound note. Sure, they run on a 220-volt system, and that can cause you to sit up with a start on personal contact with it, but the British use triple protection or more. A simple device like a blender has its own fuse; the plug has a built-in fuse; the wall socket has a fuse in it. And all that is connected through a fuse box out in the garage. The Queen herself must have once gotten a shock from her electric bed warmer to warrant all that codified redundancy.

In our bathroom the only electrical concession to modern convenience sat over the sink. There must be a regulation in this country that proscribes creative bathroom lighting. Every bathroom we've seen in this country, in homes or hotels, has the same art-deco fixture over the mirror.

The white enameled box with a rippled glass lens had a pull switch with a short string. Next to the switch a small outlet had a label that admonished "shavers only." Along side a toggle switch inexplicably allowed a choice of 220 or 110. I pondered why all the bathrooms of Great Britain would have outlets for 110-volt American shavers.

"I guess we're not plugging the heater into that."

While British electrical codes might dictate the most exacting details, British carpentry leaves abundant room to maneuver. Not a door in our house reached down to the threshold, so it was a trifle to run the power cord out to the bedroom.

The next day we enjoyed a warm steamy bathroom all the way through our morning toilets, ever wary, however, that an inspector from the RBP might seize upon us any minute and confiscate our contraband device.

January 3

Dear Richard,

The Christmas swap party was a hoot. After all that fussing and concern about behavior and hurt feelings, they were ruthless. They tossed gifts on the floor in feigned disgust and stole from another on their turns, which led to much wailing and breast beating. I think the secret was the long cocktail hour before we started.

The string of Christmas lights that we put around our front door lasted only two days past the party before someone "nicked" them. The last laugh is on them, though. They were American lights and will only work here on a transformer that costs about £16. It did give us an idea about what to do with our Christmas tree since we were going away for the whole holiday. The night before we left we put the tree by the gate in front of the house. As we left the next morning, we noticed it was gone. Peace on earth and good will to men.

I noticed there were no scones on the shelf at the supermarket the last two times I was there. I asked and they told me that they had so much trouble keeping the scones in stock that they've discontinued them. Honest. That's what they said.

The merchants of Claygate have prevailed on the police to allow parking on both sides of the street. That leaves only one lane down the middle of the long parade of stores. I got caught in the ultimate gridlock when I met a car coming the other way. Both of us were followed by five or six other cars and all dozen came to a dead stop. But no horns blared, no one shouted. The fellow in front of me got out and maneuvered all the cars into parking spaces so that soon we could make our way past them. Patience was invented in Britain. Since I have not quite acquired it, I came home and had a cup of tea, which I understand is the eleventh and next to last step.

TJDGI # 11: Our supermarket had a special, three French bread baguettes for £1.17. I took one, expecting to pay 39 p. "No ma'am. The special is only if you buy three. Otherwise they cost 59 p each." I was going to ask her if I would have to pay £1.18 if I bought two, but I'm trying to be a nice American.

Love, and on my best behavior, your sister

Bill Leffler

13

Foxes

On an unseasonably muggy Friday in February, the countryside people converged on the center of London, and the Labour Government engaged in its latest crisis. A Member of Parliament, a "bleeding-heart, anti-vivisectionist, disestablishment liberal," according to Alistair, had introduced a bill which would outlaw fox hunting. Three nights later the Prime Minister himself had announced his support for the bill.

I was there only because I had been caught in a taxi between appointments near Hyde Park Corner. I watched thousands debark from buses and gush out of the tube station. Some, heavy with sweat, were dressed in loden tweed, woolen kneesocks, and three-penny caps. A few men in button-topped riding hats, red hunting coats, and white breeches congregated in small, animated groups. The slapped their thighs continually with leather croups, as if they desperately wanted to be astride their horses, ready to gallop at the sound of the horn. Some carried placards, lambasting the government for threatening Their Freedom, Their Way of Life, Their Livelihoods, and even the Very Soul of England.

At a site not far from the Corner, the Countryside Alliance, the organizing group behind all this, had erected a grand stage and podium. A procession of recognizably important people and charismatic speakers urged solidarity. They dispatched a mission to 10 Downing Street with dramatic fanfare.

This was no ragtag march of peasants with pitchforks, clubs, and torches in search of a British bastille. They looked mostly like ordinary people that you might meet walking along the streets of Chertsey or Stowe-on-Wold. Some had come from as far as Wales and Scotland by train or bus. In a land obsessed with unemployment remedies, they came to tell their government that fox hunting was about jobs, not animal cruelty.

My image of fox hunting comes from old lithographs and their modern renderings on pub placemats. Most were done by artists who never quite mastered three dimensions. The Earl of Snottingly and other red-coated gentry, atop improbably tall white steeds, preened cavalierly or leapt rock walls in a single bound. In the distance, which in their flat world sat only two inches to the left, a pack of dogs raced up a hill pursuing a hapless fox, running desperately to save his tail.

In contrast, the stories told by these congregated country folk and reported in the *Evening Standard* painted a picture of stableboys, groomsmen, and kennel managers; of leathermen, blacksmiths, and veterinarians; of haberdashers, caterers, and butchers. In addition, they had dragged with them their natural allies, the cadre that supports the pheasant shoots and angling. Along came the beaters, the fly-tiers, the fishmongers, the pluckers, the sports shop owners, the nurserymen, and hatcherymen. In sum, the throngs that milled around Hyde Park that day were indeed the Ordinary Folk of Britain.

That night we had the good fortune to attend a small dinner party in the Close given by Curt and Marie-Hèléne. Curt pronounces her name MAH-ray-eh-LAIN. I have slipped and called her Mary Lynn only once. Their dinner parties are a Close legend - Marie-Hélène as the gourmet chef, Curt as the epicure of fine wine.

Even a casual invitation in this country had a protocol. The hand written note asked us to arrive "at 20:00 for 20:30..." Was this an admonition "to show up early so you don't keep us waiting??"

Au contraire. In this case it meant Curt plied us with a Veuve Cliquot Ponsardin '93 Brut, a treat not to be taken indifferently, while Marie-Hèléne fed us Swedish salmon with *crème fraîch* on little blintzes she had made not an half hour earlier.

Besides Curt (Welsh) and Marie-Hèléne (French), two Swedes and but one Englishman joined we token Americans. Accordingly our hosts continued their subtly international flavor for the evening with their menu of crispy roast grouse, some succulent but otherwise unidentifiable Iberian tubers and, incredibly enough, pan-fried okra. Curt ceremoniously filled our glasses from a decanter of Sarget du Chateau Gruad Larose '86, as best my faltering memory of that night can recall.

When Curt finally settled in next to me I asked him why he had transferred the wine out of its own bottle. Anxious to flaunt my recent mastery of decanting, I told him I thought only port needed separation from its crusty sediment. "Why would one decant wine?"

Deep furrows appeared above his bushy eyebrows. His voice turned authoritative. "This particular vintage is quite slow to reveal itself. As I splash the wine into the decanter, intimate mixing with air allows the full bouquet to open, particularly the hints of cherry and vanilla.

In a lower voice he continued, "And besides, drinking still wine makes me fart."

Like the afternoon, the evening was unseasonably warm. As Marie-Héléne served after dinner sweets of meringue and berries, followed by cheese and biscuits, Curt opened the French doors of the dining room to their fine English garden. A grass carpet abutted beds of red and white blossoms in front of walls of dense privet. I half-expected Puck to bound onto the floodlit landscape and deliver the opening lines to *A Midsummer's Night Dream*. (I have already explained the limits to my knowledge of Shakespeare, but we had just seen *Dream* performed in Tunbridge Wells the week before.) Instead, to my surprise, onto center stage walked a four-legged, dog-sized creature with pointy ears and bushy red tail.

"Is that a fox?" I asked.

"Oh yes, she's lived here for a while," said Marie-Héléne. "She had a litter of pups a few weeks ago. They were a marvelous sight, tumbling across the garden."

"But a fox? Is it tame? Do you feed it?"

"Oh once in a while, on the occasions when she presents herself."

"Probably get the mange from it," grumbled Curt. "Or our dogs will. They'll probably die from it. Not all that bad, I suppose."

"Oh posh Curt, they will not."

Before such a tranquil night collapsed in domestic shambles, I seized a moment to steer the conversation to earlier today. "I don't understand all the uproar this morning and in the press today about foxes and fox hunting. Matter of fact, I don't even understand fox hunting. What's the object of that sport anyway? How do you win?"

"You bloody well stay on your horse, that's how," volunteered Julian, the English guest. Julian sported nothing but proper attire for this occasion. Dark suit, cuff-linked blue shirt with a white collar. Or was it a white shirt with a blue collar? His school tie had the stripes descending right to left. ("Goes back to the chivalrous times and the evocative epithet, 'from the heart to the sword'," Alistair had explained to me. "If you bought the same tie in America, the stripes would go down from left to right. Some English gent had an American tailor make one up for him, the story goes, but he described it after looking in the mirror and bollixed it. You Yanks never got it right after that.")

"'Bloody well' is the right expression," said Lillie, the Swedish diner. "It's barbaric what they do to those foxes. Prince Charles and the rest of that crowd should be ashamed of their behavior."

"To the contrary, Lillie. I rather think you don't quite understand how important a symbol fox hunting is to England. It is one of the few remnants of civility in a world where authenticity is rapidly disappearing. And it has little to do with aristocracy. It is quite egalitarian. "

"It surprises me you should say that," I offered. "I thought you would have to own a manor house in the

Cotswolds and a townhouse in Mayfair to qualify for a fox hunt."

"Not at all. I'm going on a foxhunt myself tomorrow in New Forest. The huntmaster happens to be the greengocer in Burley. Half the riders will be from the town."

"But what about the way they brutalize the fox when they catch it," said Lillie, frowning as though she had just sucked a dill pickle.

"First of all, do you realize how much destruction foxes do in the countryside. They terrorize the wild fowl. They devastate the domestic chick population. Secondly, hunting with horse and hound to control the fox population is as close as possible to the natural order. Would your rather traps be set or poison be left in the wood?"

"I'd rather you just leave them be."

"And forgo the grouse we had for dinner tonight?"

The conversation started to sound acrimonious, but Curt, the perfect host, broke in to lead us to the sitting room for snifters of Hennessey and Godiva chocolates.

"Would any of you fancy joining me on tomorrow's hunt?" asked Julian. "You'll have the chance to see for yourselves that fox hunting is quite civilized and isn't all about arrogant gentry, intimidating the local peasants by trampling their fields and ruining their crops, ending with ruthless slaughter of an innocent."

"Actually the last part sounds like it might be exciting," I said. "But I'd go for a chance for either one."

"Splendid. Do you ride, or would you rather walk?"

"Walk? How can you walk a fox hunt?"

"Actually, walking is rather popular way to participate. I would venture that several score or so will follow on foot. Most can't afford a horse, especially the townspeople, so they walk or drive to strategic sites along the usual hunt path and wait and watch. The sound of the hounds and the horn will guide them. So which will it be? Horseback or foot? I can line up a mount easily enough."

I glanced at Eileen, hoping she would encourage me to walk. Lingering memories of my flight from the moors astride Charger flashed before me. "Don't look at me for support," she said. "You're on your own tomorrow."

"Well I'm sure I'd embarrass myself with the clothes I'd have to wear." Now that I had put myself out on point, I grasped at excuses to renege.

"Not really a problem," said Julian. "I have a set of rat-catchers that will fit you."

"That doesn't exactly sound like the bright red uniform I'm used to seeing in the hunting prints."

"Oh no," said Julian. "Rat-catchers are worn by the new-comers and young children. Woolen breeches and a tweed jacket, leather riding boots, and oh, you must have a somber tie to wear. Most of the riders will be in black hunting coats. The full colors – scarlet in our case – are reserved for the masters and servants.

Curt jumped in. "And you can tell the difference by the number of gold buttons on their coats," he said with an amused smile.

"Sounds deplorably hierarchical," said Lillie.

"Well, think about it. Hunting is one of the few pursuits in this country where proper dress is compulsory," Julian said, reaching full gallop in his effort to convince the group. "Despite what I said about foxes being a nuisance, hunting really has passed beyond being a necessity to society. It is now more ceremonial, a symbol of leisure and freedom. But costumes are an important part of it."

Julian's face had reddened and he started to splutter. Spittle filled the air with every word containing a hard *p*. "Appropriate apparel shows respect to the farmers over whose land we ride. Separates us from the barbarians, makes us part of a society that shows respect for rules and hierarchy."

I raised my cognac into the moist atmosphere. "To liberty, equality, and fraternity. Fox hunting by horse it is."

Curt met my glass with his. "A toast to civilization," he said, and nodding at me with a mildly cynical smile, "and may you still be in the saddle after the first fence."

****

At 7:30 the next morning, Julian tooted the horn of his Vauxhall roadster at our front gate. With my wellies under my arm and the gorge from my stomach heading somewhere north of my esophagus, we set off for the New Forest.

"Good morning, sport. Your costume is in the back seat," he said, thumbing at a tumble of leather and woolens. "You'll probably not have use for those wellies, being in the saddle all the while."

I hoped that he would be right about "all the while."

As we raced through the gray drizzle down the Portsmouth Road, Julian resumed his *Apologia pro venatus vulpis*.

"Last night you mentioned your tea-tray image of fox hunting. The real nature of the dress code is universally misunderstood. The costume, be it the six-button red coat of the Huntmaster or that ruddy outfit in the back is really a uniform. Even more, an insignia of office. The hunt dress code creates order out of chaos. Rank and equality at the same time. During the hunt, civilian income and status have no meaning, only the rank in the 'field.' "

Julian was revving faster than his Vauxhall, but the whine of the tires on the wet pavement competed for my attention.

"The egalitarians would do away with all this in their misguided alliance with the *animalia aequitas*. God knows a foxhunting ban would be just another domino in the overdevelopment of the countryside. And would they have us trade the horse and hound for shotguns and gases to control the fox ...

I awoke abruptly to tires scratching on gravel and the smell of manure. We were pulling into a stable yard filled with mounted horses and scores of attendees.

"Who are all these people?" I asked Julian.

"Good morning again. I'm afraid I may have run on a bit. Those are the groomsmen, the stableboys, and the men from the saddlery and the ironmonger's. All the attendees of the riders. I see the main part of the hunt has already departed. Ah, there's the stable owner. I'll collect our horses and you change your outfit in that stable. We're the tiniest bit tardy."

The knickers and baggy jacket went on easily enough, complementing my tattersall shirt and conservative brown tie. For four or five minutes I struggled to pull on the riding boots, working up a sweat and adding my own scent to the *eau de equine* of the rat-catchers. By the time I returned to the yard, Julian had already mounted his horse.

"Righty-ho," he said. "Here's your horse."

I looked around and saw no animal that wasn't already being ridden. Julian saw the question mark on my face. "Here. Over here." He was pointing to the other side of his horse. "This is Tawny," he said, as if he were introducing me to a blind date.

Tawny was indeed your worst-nightmare blind date. She stood a foot shorter than Julian's horse. Tawny may have once been a chestnut filly, giving rise to her name, but now she sported a mouse-brown coat and opaque eyes that attested to a score of years in front of a plough or haywagon. I must say, however, that in a post-Charger world, this spectacle of weatherworn horseflesh suited me just fine.

As we headed down Eyeworth Pond Lane to the Village of Burley, Tawny and I fell in behind Julian without the slightest prompt on my part. In the car park of the Forester Inn, the hunt had assembled in a wonderfully bucolic collage of man, beast, and woodland.

"Brief me again about all the different riding costumes," I said behind my hand to Julian. "I see black coats, some red; some have green collars, some black. How do I know who to follow and who to stay away from?"

"If you end up not behind me ... well, someone no doubt advise you soon enough. Do you see the Huntmaster there?" Julian pointed to the most distinguished of the riders. He sported five gold buttons on his black-collared red coat. Paradoxically spoiling his lithographic pose was the cell phone he talked into.

"Stay well behind him."

Tawny, I noticed, was starting to become a little agitated, stamping her feet, and snorting like horses do. Maybe it was the pack of hounds not 30 feet from us that were in their own state of nervous anticipation, standing up, sitting down, turning in circles, and peeing. The Whipper-in, a scowling redcoat, trotted back and forth, keeping them pressed against the car park fence.

"Here comes the collection," said Julian. "You might want to make a small contribution to the Forester for their treats."

A lady in tweeds worked her way through the crowd with a small velvet poke, accepting donations from the riders and pedestrians. With some effort I retrieved from my pocket three one pound coins and on my turn received a hardy thank you from her. Just behind her came four men in servants' attire with trays of steaming cups. I accepted one that turned out to be a mixture of gin and grape juice with bits and pieces of floating fruit.

From a second passing tray I picked another treat, a sweet sausage baked into the middle of a filo crust. As I munched on it, I noticed a young rider nearby, eyeing me with some disdain as she tasted hers. She was in perfect ensemble – freshly pressed jacket and scarf, lily-white breeches, and boots with a patent leather shine. Her blond braided hair reached down her back to the saddle.

191

She sat on an imposing horse, a statuesque beast that could rouse a Greek sculptor from the tomb. The grooms had ribboned its mane. They had shaved its midsection nearly clean of hair. Beyond the scalloped border with the hindsection, they had brushed the coat over its rippling muscles to a copper sheen. In inspiring symmetry, they had braided its tail to match its young rider's. If that horse had dropped a big patty in the middle of the car park, no one would have noticed because it definitely wouldn't stink.

In my interminable effort to spread American charm abroad, I made eye contact with the girl and asked, holding up the snack, "What do you suppose these little buggers are?"

I had momentarily forgotten that in Britain, *bugger* has a special meaning. She showed the full whites of her eyes in a look of shock, then tossed her head in the other direction, sniffed, and spurred her horse away. So much for diplomatic endeavors.

Blessedly in a few moments the Huntmaster gave the signal. The whipper-in ordered the hounds into action. The whole troop moved off toward the woods behind the dogs. Two inappropriately scruffy fellows at the side picked up their placards and got ready to fall in behind.

"Who are they?" I asked Julian.

"The tree-huggers? It's the RSPC. They harass almost every hunt."

"How do they keep up?"

"They'll have spotters through the field. See, there's one of them on his mobile now."

The one with the greasier beard and tangled hair juggled a cell phone and placard. I got close enough as we passed by to see the message on his sign. A close up black and white picture of two dogs tearing at a mutilated fox had the caption,

ALL THOSE IN FAVOUR OF BANNING
FOX HUNTING RAISE YOUR HANDS
or lower your heads

A score of pedestrians fell in behind, all of them in their tweeds and wellies. Another 30 or 40 went for their cars, heading to the crossing points, perhaps to harass the harassers.

Tawny fell in without hesitation. Her ears were now pricked as she all but pranced down the road. Twenty minutes into the woods, the parade had fallen well behind the hounds when the Huntmaster signaled us to stop. From across the glen yelps and howling began as the hounds got onto a scent. A few toots from a huntsman's horn signaled something important. Tawny stamped and snorted continuously.

The raised hand of the Huntmaster came down to the shouts of "Tally-ho" as the group moved out. I held on desperately as Tawny leapt forward in a spasm of uncontrollable excitement. Off the path and across the meadow the pack charged. The noise of the 45 horses pounding the earth drowned the sound of the baying hounds.

Somehow I was never able to communicate my intentions to Tawny. I would have been content to follow along at measured pace and watch the experienced riders perform. Even ancient in horse years as she was, Tawny could not be content as a lurker. This horse had become a ton of seething flesh with the thrill of the hunt now coursing through her blood vessels. To my alarm I began to realize she was not even a follower. Tawny began to surge past the others, squeezing between the haunches of horses four hands higher than she. I smiled wanly at their riders as I overtook them. Within a few minutes we were within reach of the front of the pack as it splashed through a swale, made boggy by last night's rain.

Water flew everywhere. Manicured horsehair and impeccable white breeches became sodden with mud. I took strange delight in seeing the young blond brat wipe a brown glob from the side of her face as if it were fecal matter. But then she pointed her nose up again and kicked her horse ahead.

Tawny, only briefly slowed by the ooze, resumed her determination to reach the vanguard. Over the tumult I heard the quavering sound of the huntsman's horn again. The Huntmaster turned the formation sharply to the right. To my horror I saw a dry-stone wall between the sound and us. The Huntmaster rushed the wall and cleared it easily.

Jumping, I found out, has varying degrees of risk, especially if the leap is not successfully high enough. A wooden fence, in that case, will probably give way, unable to withstand the momentum of more than a ton of horse and human flesh. Hedgerows give way too, although not without contusion and abrasion. But a dry-stone wall presents an immovable object to an otherwise irresistible force.

Tawny understood none of this. In a surge of elemental gusto, she raced towards the wall as I watched a dozen others ahead of us clear it. With not one clue what my role was in this impending act of lunacy, I leaned forward, grabbed the saddle front, and let Tawny have her head. Five meters in front of the wall she went airborne, cutting off a redcoat who reined his horse to the right of us, firing a salvo of verbal abuse.

For an indefinite period, Tawny and I glided, first in suspended animation, with the drywall passing dreamily underneath us. Then came free fall, at which point I became increasingly aware that the leap is only half the hazard – landing is the remainder. Tawny's abrupt contact with the ground occurred at the moment that I hovered six inches above the saddle. Over her head I vaulted. My only recollection for the next few moments was the snot-nosed twelve year-old, smirking as she bounded by.

After a quick inventory of my extremities, I realized that lush wet grass and mud had cushioned my ignoble landing. I rolled over to one side to let 20 or 30 more riders carry on, chasing Tawny who had not paused a moment in her quest for the lead.

Within a few moments a horse and rider appeared that seemed to have been catapulted over the wall. The rider flailed at the air in a vain attempt to right the two of them. Horse and rider crashed to the ground, he skidding ten meters to my feet. The horse got up awkwardly and with an embarrassed look, trotted off in the direction of the others. The body in front of me lay deathly still.

"Are you okay?" I tried.

"Bugger all if I know." Ah, that b-word again. "But I suppose we'll survive, what?" came the answer from the motionless form

He rolled over, slowly and carefully. "No sense whinging over spilt milk. Or should I say a spilt rider. Desmond Manning," he said, holding out his hand.

We sat for a while, taking nips of sloe gin from the silver flask he carried with him, talking about the hunt and falling from horses. Shortly someone whose role I never understood came walking across the meadow with Tawny and Desmond's horse in tow. Tawny was lathered in sweat. Her head hung in front of her as if she knew she had completed her last hunt and was earmarked as tomorrow's main course for the hounds. And that might well have been true.

The hunt lasted over four hours. In the softest chair I could find at the Forester I waited for Julian to return.

"Well, was the hunt a success? Did you nab the fox?" I asked him when he arrived.

"Indeed we did, not ten furlongs from here. Quite a hunt. I must have lost almost a stone, but this will help," he said, as I handed him a pint of Young's Bitter.

"What happens to the fox when you finally get to him? Do the dogs really tear him apart? Or do you tree him and shoot him? Or what?"

"Actually, you'd probably rather not know. Really."

******

Three weeks later I read in *The Times* that the House of Commons remanded the "Private Member's Bill to Ban Hunting with Dogs" to committee for further consideration. Parliament had preserved this piece of English heritage for at least one more year.

Bill Leffler

February 25

Dear Richard,

We're trying, but we can't fit it all in. We spent the weekend in Kent at a B&B made from a converted oast house, an old hops-drying barn. The proprietress no doubt came from Teutonic lineage. "You must tell me now what you want for breakfast. I go to bed quite early," she said, almost the moment we arrived. A while later, as we left for the day, "Parking lights only when you arrive back tonight. Park away from the building." The next morning, she barked at me at breakfast. "Don't sit *there*. That's a chair for a man. Sit *there*." She pointed to an identical chair, but on the long side of the table. Bill hurried to take the man's seat. When she left he whispered to me, nodding towards the window, "Notice that we're the only car in the car park this morning." While we ate, she stared disapprovingly at me as I slathered preserves on my scone. Finally she blurted out, "You're not going to have enough left for the toast." (And vee vill eat the toast, ja?) Luckily, the B&B was otherwise charming.

Saturday afternoon we were exploring the town and heard the church bells ringing fiercely. We stopped in and saw six people under the belfry bobbing up and down on ropes, to the direction of a seventh. They played three different pieces – I wouldn't call them songs – but we couldn't tell them apart. We mentioned to der B-und-B Meister how pleasant the bellringing sounded and she retorted, "You think so now. They're practicing for the interchurch pealing competition to be held here tomorrow afternoon. Twelve teams from all over Kent clanging those bloody bells for six hours. Altogether preposterous. We're buggering off before it starts. You'll have to as well." Ja wohl, mein Fraulein.

198

The first elimination rounds of the tennis championships started this weekend. Lulu and I made it past the first three matches, beating two of our own D team pairs and one of the A Team. Next week is the showdown. The Doe has suddenly become all sweetness with us. Invited us to join her for tea. Lulu declined, "I have a cyst on my bum that needs attention," leaving the Doe with a puzzled look on her face. Wish us luck.

TJDGI #11: The wonderful castles that lie along the Dee River in Scotland are open to the public on weekends. We arrived at the first and most massive, Drum Castle, at 10 a.m. The guard told us all the castles open at 1:30. We decided it would be efficient to start at the other end of the Royal Deeside Road so we drove 70 miles west, past a half dozen other castles to Balmoral, which had a sign at the gate, SORRY, NOT OPEN TO THE PUBLIC. We detoured for lunch, then settled for a tour at the tiny Craigievar Castle a few miles away. At the tour's end they told us that all the castles close at 4 p.m. So we tore back to the first, which we thought would be the best, to find it had closed at 3:30 that day for a private function. Luckily the Deeside scenery was nice.

Love, your frantic sister

14

Planes, Trains, and Autobuses

"Your Hellcat and Bearcat, your Flying Fortress, yeh? Your P-38s, your Spitfires. There'll be several Spitfires, yeh?"

Clive wiped the accumulated saliva from the corners of his mouth. He struggled to keep his hands on the wheel as his enthusiasm filled the car. "There'll have them all there this weekend at Croydon. Royal Air Force base there. Yeh? Commemorating the fiftieth anniversary of the first kill by a Spitfire. The lady who owns that plane will be flying it at the show. Yeh? Can you believe that? She's flying for her husband who restored that plane to air worthy. But he died and she took over. Yeh? And another chap who owns the Spitfire that was in on the second kill will be flying too."

Like anyone I ever met from the Midlands, Clive checked with me every two or three thoughts (Yeh?) and peeked in the rearview mirror to be sure I got it. We were driving down the M-4 from Heathrow towards home in Surrey. People who fly in and out of Heathrow soon learn that it's cheaper to have a driver pick them up and take them home than it is to park anywhere near the airport. And what a treat it always was to have a chauffeur pick me up at 6:15 on a Wednesday morning and fight the commuter traffic for me and be waiting at Heathrow on at 6:00 on Friday night to do the same thing.

I mentioned to Clive that I had once visited the Royal Air Force Museum one free afternoon during a business trip. "Oh, brilliant place. Lovely," he said. "I got lucky one time when I went there. They were testing the engine on a Fokker. Yeh? They let me stand right there while they did it. I had my son with me to share the thrill. Couldn't believe the noise coming from that Fokker. Yeh? Another time they were getting a Bearcat ready for its air test. Yeh? That was really exciting."

I had talked to another driver, Doug, just the week before who had just as much passion about trains as Clive did for planes. I told Clive about that and asked him, "Are these air shows more or less like the trainspotting your buddy Doug did?"

"Never could see it," Clive said. "Them trainspotters went down to Paddington Station and sat on a bench all day and wrote down train numbers, just to fill up their books. Sounded daft to me."

"I trainspotted when I was a lad," Doug had told me. "All my mates did. We had books listing the serial numbers of every steam engine in service and we'd check off each one as we saw it. Then we'd compare them with each other and get clues where we could find engines we hadn't checked off yet. A young lad could start out at his local train station, but soon he'd have to move on to an interchange. I was lucky because I lived near Clapham Junction, which is still Britain's busiest. I could spend day after day there and still see engines I hadn't logged in before."

"So what did you do with the books when you got them all checked off?" I asked him.

"Oh, we never did fill one up. Not quite like your baseball cards. We couldn't go to the candy store and buy more or trade them with our mates to fill up a set. We had to actually spot them ourselves. But we did develop a kind of currency. We'd trade secrets with each other. We'd tell each other 'Go down the mainline to the Tripechips Cutoff and find the spur that runs towards the River Mole. Go about 700 meters past the bracken-covered mill and you'll see another rusty sidetrack. A hundred meters down there you'll find a No. 555 Lambton 0-6-2T from the Coal Board Collieries.' We'd have to give up something to get that kind of intelligence, but then we'd have something tradable ourselves."

"But why all this enthusiasm for spotting trains, Doug?" I asked him.

"You probably don't know how different those times were. I'm talking about the forties and fifties. Nobody in Britain had two shillings to rub together after the war. I can remember my mum waking me up on winter mornings. The temperature in the house would be four degrees outside and eight inside. I had to haul the coal scuttle about two miles to the coal yard and buy enough fuel to keep the house warm for a day or two. Even if we could have afforded more, we had to have a ration coupon from the government. Same thing with food. Walk to the market every day and shop. Every day, because we couldn't carry more than that. Had to walk, because we didn't know anyone who owned a car. Didn't matter, though. Petrol was rationed too. "

"And that made everyone want to be a trainspotter?"

"Quite. The book only cost six pence. No admission to the train station. And plenty of exercise following a derelict spur and sidetrack to its terminus. Perfect for an 11 year-old lad."

"Do you still have all your logs?" I asked Doug.

"Oh, I think mum tossed them when we moved house one time," he said wistfully.

It might be, in the Big Scheme of Things, that a checkmark next to a No. 6024 King Edward 4-6-0 from the Swindon Works was the equivalent of a Mickey Mantle rookie card. In that case trainspotting really was the same as collecting baseball cards, the pastime of every red-blooded America youth. And every year across America and Britain, while spring cleaning their empty nests, moms guilelessly tossed in the trash priceless collections of cards and log books.

The steam engine disappeared from the mainlines of Britain in the 1960's. In a burst of progressive efficiency British Rail replaced coal with diesel fuel and made redundant both the stoker and the romantic era. Still, once a month Doug goes to an evening meeting of Railroaders, where old trainspotters meet. They watch slide shows of each other's train trips in Wales or Canterbury where the few steam engines left haul tourists seven miles from one souvenir shop to another.

Electric commuter trains had their own curious nostalgia. British Rail had also long ago converted all the commuter trains to electric power. Despite this quantum advance in technology, on many lines the rolling stock dates back more than half a century and decades of bureaucratic parenthood have exacted a toll on reliability. On my first commute to London, I waited interminably on a misty platform for the 7:28 to arrive. Every few minutes someone would take a large bite of a scone and then make an entirely incomprehensible announcement over the p.a. system. I asked the commuter standing next to me what he said.

"Oh something about some delays near Guilford. Maybe there's leaves on the tracks again."

"Leaves?"

"Happens first rain every autumn. Leaves fall on the third rail and break contact with the train. Then the trainman has to go out and clean them off to get the train going again."

"You're kidding me."

"No. Wait till the winter when we sometimes get the 'wrong kind of snow' on the rails. Then we might have to wait for an hour or two to get in."

About 7:50, the Train That Time Forgot trudged into the station. I followed my cynical companion as he turned the steel handle and swung open one of the eight doors along the car in front of us. We stumbled haplessly between the six passengers facing each other on bench seats inside the door. Newspapers fell to the floor and coffee in paper cups sloshed about. I followed him past the center aisle and plopped down on a bench seat across the car. I looked up to see the six commuters I had wriggled past glaring at me.

"We'll go mate, as soon as someone shuts the door."

Wholly mortified, I got up to mash my way back to the door, which had by then swung all the way out, flush to the outside of the car. "I'll get it," the outboard passenger grumbled, and he reached around and swung the door shut with a thunderous clap I could feel in my teeth.

"Slam door trains, we call them," Alistair told me later. "If you stand on the platform and watch the full length of the train, you hear the slam-slam-slam as they swing the doors shut. Reminds me of field artillery when they fire volleys down the line."

Besides the commuter trains, intercity passenger trains that ply the longer routes are, for the most part, paragons of modernity, all steel, glass, and vinyl fittings. But a few are still only a step above those Victorian meat wagons that haul commuters to and from their jobs. I rode the London to Norwich train one day, en route to the town of Lowestoft on the East Coast. Gaylor, our on-site manager, had joined me and was bemoaning his inability to organize a petition for a free trade zone. He needed to consolidate the commercial interests of two cities, Norwich and Great Yarmouth. "Perennially at odds with each other. Different political backgrounds. One supported Cromwell and the other the Royalists. And when the monarchy was restored under Charles II, Great Yarmouth was given the herring concession. The people of Lowestoft haven't forgotten."

"Wait a minute. Wasn't that a long time ago?"

"1650. But these people don't readily accept change."

Gaylor and I finished a bottle of cheap Cote du Rhone while awaiting a late supper on the Norwich Express's dining car. From the tantalizingly complete menu I had ordered the Boeuf Bourguignon and he the

Chicken Kiev. As he poured the last drops in to our plastic wineglasses, a sullen attendant delivered our entrees, steaming hot but still in their microwaveable plastic containers. With diminished relish and some dismay, Gaylor enounced, "That definitely calls for another bottle of red." I immediately adjourned to the Gentleman's WC in preparation.

Nostalgia is where you find it, including in a wood-paneled lavatory of a vintage train. Over the toilet hung a brass plaque, tarnished with age, which sent me back to radio days – Sunday nights in my living room at age ten, listening to a new Danish comedian/pianist, Victor Borge. I had held my sides and laughed as he performed a love song set to the music of *Humoresque*. He claimed unconvincingly that the inspiration for the ditty came during a recent train ride in Britain. But now in brass letters above the commode, I read, "Customer will please refrain from flushing toilets while the train is in the station," to which Borge added, "Darling, I love you." Then he continued. "We encourage constipation while the train is in the station, moonlight always makes me think of you."

All these years I was sure Borge had made up the whole thing. But there it was, British Rail admonishing me not to foul Liverpool Station by taking a dump right in front of the platform.

On another chauffeured trip down the M-4 towards home, I asked Doug if he know of the Autobus Museum. "Oh, the one near Weybridge? I've taken the wife and kids there. Good fun."

I had seen scores of cars full of people descend on the place one Sunday afternoon as we played golf at the adjacent course along the River Wey. Double-decker buses of all kinds dominated the open air museum, but even the regular suburban and intercity buses had people crawling all over them, sitting in the seats with dreamy faces. "Look Sid. There's the Tooting to Holbern local," they'd yell to each other. I had a hard time thinking of myself saying to the family on Sunday, "Hey gang. Let's all go down to the bus museum this afternoon. They've just acquired a 1950 Leyland PS2 48 seater from Yorkshire. And East Anglia has lent them a '48 Rotherham Gritwagon."

"You probably like to look at antique cars," Doug said, "You have to remember that buses were the only form of transportation available to most of us back then."

Duly reproached, I thought to myself, he's right and when I was a kid, I didn't have to haul a bucket of coal two miles in the snow every morning, probably uphill in both directions ...

One lunch hour I walked the three blocks down the Strand from my office to the London Transport Museum because I still didn't understand this preoccupation with planes, trains, and buses. Inside I wandered past an old double-decker bus, a recreated tube station, and a locomotive of unknown vintage. I passed two chaps in front of a bookstand, thumbing through <u>Reg Wilson's Municipal Buses in Colour 1959-74</u> and <u>The Yorkshire Bus Handbook.</u> I stopped and counted a selection of 254 of similarly enticing titles to choose from.

In the back corner of the museum a grainy black and white film ran continuously, documenting the demise of the London tram system. Trams ran on tracks all over this city at one time, powered through their electric umbilicals from overhead lines. I took a seat in the last row and watched as they showed a couple board one for its last run, he in his dark suit and fedora, she in her flower-print dress and kerchief. They just rode holding hands as the announcer droned on about the collapse of the network. The closing shots showed the tracks being paved over and the wooden carcasses of the cars being irreverently trashed and incinerated.

Only one other patron watched this wistful saga, a little old man in the front row in a frayed suit and timeworn hat. His intense interest captured everything I needed to know about this pervasive preoccupation with transportation, and perhaps, if I can trifle with the dramatic, even the national character. For all I knew, this dolefully frail figure might have been the man in the movie, now alone, remembering the thrill of paying a tuppence for a tram ride on a Sunday afternoon. Perhaps he was taking his wife to Hyde Park Corner to listen to the soapbox orators; or to the banks of the Thames River for a picnic; or maybe they simply were going to the pub for Sunday Roast in an era, a more civilized time, the rest of us have almost forgotten.

March 26

Dear Richard,

They tried every thing – bad line calls, confusing the score, medical time-outs, long strategy conferences. But we beat them in three sets, 3-6, 6-3, and 7-5. The Doe is dead. Long live the new Doe. Lulu immediately went into the locker room and put on her gold jewelry, stuck her butt out, and strutted back to the grill for all the congratulations. The old Doe had already left in disgrace. I'm so happy I can leave Lulu behind as the champ. I'll miss her.

I thought I had it all down pat. Our last visitors, Kaye and Joanne, just left. After the usual turn-around at Hampton Court Palace, I took them into London. This time I chose to ride in a first class railcar, with its individual compartments and plush seats. As we pulled into our destination, Wimbledon Station, I saw to my horror there was a steel plate where the door handle should be. While I panicked, Kaye read the faded instructions on the door that directed us to slide down the window, reach out, and turn the handle on the outside, slide the window back up, and swing the door open. Now surely that qualifies as TJDGI # 12.

The removal company is coming for our stuff in three days but what a terrible week to be leaving this wonderful country. Blue skies and balmy breezes. I walked into town today and saw the crocus, iris, and daffodils peaking out of the ground in Esher Green. Weather was the topic on every corner. "Yes, isn't it lovely today?" "Yes, lovely." But at the supermarket I heard an elderly lady mumbling to herself. I asked if I could help her. "Oh no, dear. I just hate this store." I tried to convince her it wasn't so bad. They have almost everything almost all the time and the help is friendly – in their own way. "It's not that," she said.

"Before this place opened there used to be all the nice little shops where everybody knew my name. Now they're all shut down, gone, replaced by estate agent offices and this dreadful supermarket." What could I reply to that?

Collectively Bill and I have gained more than a stone since we've been here so we decided a diet was in order before we left. I went over to Claygate to get some fresh vegetables for dinner. When I walked in the little market, the counter lady spotted me and called out, "Oh Mrs. Leffler. Good news. We have scones today."

See you soon.

Love, your sentimental sister

Bill Leffler

Acknowledgements

To my wife, Eileen, for letting me use with impunity her numerous letters back to America and for her constant encouragement.

To Kelly and Peter Rodholm for their incessant coaxing to finish this work.

To our friends in Vincent Close, Alistair and Stephanie, Marie-Hèléne and Kurt (not Curt), Aunt Pat, Rod and Jan, Warwick and Juliett, and the others who made the winter warm and the summer cool, and to Rosemary, for allowing us to rent Michael Court.

To Lulu and the girls of the D team, who added vitality and charm to our lives.

To Henry, Bruce, and David, for making my time at work so much richer, and to Mike for taking a chance on me.

To Dorsey and Susan, for leading us to places where no peasants have gone before.

Bill Leffler

About the Author

Bill Leffler retired after a thirty-six year career in the oil industry that he topped off with an assignment in the London offices of his company. There he gathered the material for *Romancing the Scone.*

Dr. Leffler received his B.S. from MIT and an MBA and Ph.D from New York University. Over the years he has written numerous magazine articles, plays, and several technical books, some of which are petroleum industry standards. Presently he teaches and consults in industry and continues to write in a variety of genre.

Other books in print:
- *Petroleum Refining in Nontechnical Language* (3rd edition), 2000, Tulsa, Ok: PennWell Publishing
- Petrochemicals in Nontechnical Language (3rd edition), 2001, Tulsa, OK: PennWell Publishing 2001
- Deepwater – the Third Wave, a Nontechnical Guide, 2003, Tulsa, OK: PennWell Publishing

Illustrations at the beginning of each chapter and on the cover, are listed below. They have been graciously made available by Lindsay Nutbrown, Managing Director of The Thomas Ross Collection, of Berkshire England. I have several, fine, hand-coloured prints of some of these original etchings, all of which and many more are available from their website. For current information, see www.thomasross.co.uk

Printed in the United States
1085900001B